Praise for *Happy Successful You*

"*Happy Successful You* provides a practical and refreshing roadmap for professionals looking to unlock their full potential. Dr. Christine Lee's philosophical approach combines with real-world insights to create a book that gives you the tools to transform yourself, starting today. Drawing from her experience coaching high achievers, Dr. Lee offers straightforward and actionable guidance to discovering meaning and purpose in your work, building meaningful relationships, and thriving in any situation. If you're ready to take charge of your life and create a happier, more fulfilling career, this book is for you."

— Marshall Goldsmith, PhD
Thinkers50 #1 Executive Coach and
New York Times bestselling author of
*The Earned Life, Triggers,* and *What Got You Here Won't Get You There*

"In recent years, anyone involved in health care has undoubtedly observed an alarming uptick in professional discontent among physicians and health care providers. The reasons are myriad—loss of autonomy, increased regulatory burden, and the mandated introduction of the computerized medical record into the doctor-patient interaction, to name just a few. Regardless of the cause, the impact is the same — decreased job satisfaction and fulfillment in what should be one of the most rewarding careers.

"While there's no shortage of self-help literature claiming to hold the remedy, Dr. Lee's contribution is distinctively refreshing. Think of her as the quintessential player-coach in the field of health care. With hands-on experience in the trenches of patient care, she delivers authentic and profoundly relatable advice from her own experiences. But what truly sets this book apart is its versatility. Dr. Lee doesn't offer a cookie-cutter solution. Instead, she presents an expansive toolbox designed for introspection and self-discovery. While these tools aren't magical cures, they aid in one's pursuit of heightened personal and professional fulfillment. I found this book to be a very comprehensive resource."

— James T. McDeavitt, MD
Executive Vice President & Dean of Clinical Affairs,
Baylor College of Medicine

"What comes across in every page of this remarkable book is Dr. Christine Lee's genuine wish for her readers to flourish and thrive by setting out on a well-marked path she has laid to discovering one's life purpose. The philosophical and cultural views are signposts along the way, informing the traveler on what is important in forging a fulfilling work, family, and communal life. Brava, Dr. Lee."

— Leslie Matsukawa, MD, Psychiatrist

"I wholeheartedly recommend *Happy Successful You*, as this book is a game changer! In a world filled with distractions and noise, the book is a treasure trove of wisdom and offers practical advice and powerful insights. It is a guiding light toward a more fulfilling, purposeful, and meaningful life."

— Roger J. Zoorob, MD, MPH, FAAFP
Richard M. Kleberg Senior Professor
Chair, Department of Family & Community Medicine
Baylor College of Medicine

"*Happy Successful You* by Christine E Lee, MD, lets you think about how you can change life by providing detailed strategies. This book helps us figure out different ways of viewing life and teaches us the importance of intentional choice, providing the ultimate happy, successful, and meaningful life. This seems to be the bible for the people who seek executive coaching to improve their lives."

— Heakyung Kim, MD
Professor and Chair
Dept of Physical Medicine & Rehabilitation
Kimberly Clark Distinguished Chair in Mobility Research
University of Texas Southwestern Medical Center

"The living of life involves the pursuit of meaning to obtain personal and professional growth. *Happy Successful You* is a must-read whether you're just starting your personal development journey or looking for a fresh perspective on your current path. With a philosophical background, Dr. Lee's life lessons are invaluable in life's growth, providing excellent insights to help you understand your decisions and giving you the confidence to pursue your dreams.

"This book reminded me of Dr. Robert Solomon, who started as a medical student but changed his studies to receive master's and doctoral degrees in philosophy and psychology from the University of Michigan, where Dr. Lee attended. This experience led him to ask many philosophical questions, and I had the privilege of having those deep discussions on the meaning of life. The changes in direction in love, business, and work are not unusual, but it's the understanding of the decision that gives comfort and reassurance to pursue the path."

— Howard B. Cotler, MD, FACS, FABOS, FAAOS.
Author of *Empty Chair* and *Accelerated Recovery*

# HAPPY SUCCESSFUL YOU

Unleashing a Life of Intentional Choices, Purpose, and Meaning

## CHRISTINE E LEE, MD

Copyright © 2024 Christine E Lee, MD
All rights reserved. No part of this book may be used or reproduced in any manner without written permission from the author and publisher, except by reviewers, bloggers or other individuals who may quote brief passages, as long as they are clearly credited to the author.

Neither the publisher nor the author is engaged in rendering professional advice or services to the individual reader. The ideas and suggestions contained in this book are not intended as a substitute for professional help. Neither the author nor the publisher shall be liable or responsible for any loss or damage allegedly arising from any information or suggestion in this book.

Capucia LLC
211 Pauline Drive #513
York, PA 17402
www.capuciapublishing.com
Send questions to: support@capuciapublishing.com

Paperback ISBN: 978-1-954920-83-5
eBook ISBN: 978-1-954920-84-2
Library of Congress Control Number: 2023923170

Cover Design: Ranilo Cabo
Layout: Ranilo Cabo
Editor and Proofreader: Melissa Wuske
Book Midwife: Karen Everitt

Printed in the United States of America

Capucia LLC is proud to be a part of the Tree Neutral® program. Tree Neutral offsets the number of trees consumed in the production and printing of this book by taking proactive steps such as planting trees in direct proportion to the number of trees used to print books. To learn more about Tree Neutral, please visit treeneutral.com.

*My Wish for You*

*May you create your own meaningful life.*
*May you recognize your purpose and*
*contribute to our world.*
*May you be kind and considerate and positively*
*impact the world.*
*May you embrace the mystery of life.*
*May you feel aligned with yourself and*
*connected with others.*
*May you show up at your best and*
*as authentically as possible.*
*May you have patience and find joy in*
*everyday things.*

*May you be happy and successful every day.*

# CONTENTS

| | |
|---|---|
| **Foreword** | 1 |
| **Introduction** | 3 |
| | |
| **Part I—Reinventing You** | 7 |
| Chapter 1   Where Are You Now? | 9 |
| Chapter 2   Choosing You | 29 |
| Chapter 3   Your Awareness | 59 |
| Chapter 4   Your Authenticity | 71 |
| Chapter 5   Making Meaningful Connections | 85 |
| | |
| **Part II—Finding the Work You Want** | 103 |
| Chapter 6   The Purpose of Work | 105 |
| Chapter 7   Creating Meaning in Work | 115 |
| | |
| **Part III—Tools and Skills for Sustainability** | 127 |
| Chapter 8   Identifying and Overcoming Challenges | 129 |
| Chapter 9   Skills to Continually Grow Your Authentic Self | 145 |

**Part IV — The Ultimate Human Goal**     157
   Chapter 10  Understanding Happiness     161
   Chapter 11  Living a Happy Life     171

**Conclusion**     181
**Call to Action**     185
**Acknowledgments**     187
**References**     189
**Contact the Author**     197
**About the Author**     199

## FOREWORD

This is not just another "self-help" book, a compilation of well-worn platitudes and common sense, repackaged to look new and original. Dr. Lee has produced something quite rare: a jargon-free, widely accessible book about how to live a good life. She adeptly blends insights from her own experience as a successful physician and mother with relevant thoughts from philosophy, psychology, and sociology. Her prose is direct, bracing, and highly motivating.

Dr. Lee provides us with the tools we need to take stock of who we are, where we are going, and how we can improve the quality of our lives and the lives of those we interact with. She has a keen analytic mind, her reasoning is rigorous, and she shows how we can use our own powers of analysis to understand ourselves; but she never forgets that we are emotional beings and that the proper cultivation of the emotions is essential for good living.

As a professional philosopher, I am amazed at her grasp of complex and subtle philosophical ideas—especially those of existential thinkers like Kierkegaard, Camus, and Sartre—but just as importantly, I'm impressed by her ability to convey the heart of those ideas in an accessible way, without distorting simplification. She makes rather abstruse philosophical concepts accessible, applies them to problems of living in our world, and puts them to work in developing a coherent, systematic guide to a better, happier life.

Over and over again, as I read through the chapters of this book, I found myself saying, "Yes! Of course, that is obviously true—but it wasn't obvious to me till she said it." Above all, this book shows us how to be productively reflective, to step back and take stock of ourselves, to see ourselves in new and constructive ways. The original, literal meaning of the term *philosophy* is "love of wisdom." Wisdom requires knowledge but is more than knowledge. This book qualifies as a valuable work of philosophy because it imparts genuine wisdom, not just knowledge.

Allen Buchanan, PhD
Laureate Professor of Philosophy,
University of Arizona
Distinguished Research Fellow,
Uehiero Centre for Practical Ethics,
University of Oxford
James B. Duke Distinguished Professor
Emeritus of Philosophy
Duke University

# INTRODUCTION

It is challenging for most people to be successful and happy while working. You've likely experienced this lack of fulfillment in your work life.

Many US professionals work long hours in high-stress jobs with little agency over their present and future. If you face unrealistic expectations or deadlines and increasing variables outside your control, your efforts go unrecognized until a desired result is produced. You get lost in the work process as your life becomes dominated by work, and you need more time for yourself.

Of more than 13,000 US physicians surveyed, about 47 percent reported symptoms of burnout, with emergency medicine specialists leading the pack (Kane 2022). When I heard of this, I was compelled to know why to find out if anything could be done to prevent it. The long working hours of physicians, the countless variables outside of our control, and the life-and-death situations we must deal with are not secret. However, I was surprised to find the conditions of burnout so widespread across the profession.

The problems are broader than the medical profession. For example, a 2021 Indeed survey of 1,500

US workers found that 52 percent are in burnout, and 67 percent of all workers believe burnout worsened during the pandemic (Threlkeld 2021). In addition, the Great Resignation, the pandemic-era trend of voluntary job departures in the US (Ellerbeck 2023), there were numerous frank conversations about burnout in the media and across organizations, indicating how big the problem is. To put this in perspective, a record 50.5 million people quit their jobs in 2022, beating the 2021 record of close to 48 million, according to the US Bureau of Labor Statistics (Inacurci 2023).

A confluence of forces in our work culture and society is decoupling the essential connection between work and joy, leading to worrying levels of unhappiness. I want to help people feel motivated, satisfied, and fulfilled. Without those qualities, your dignity and well-being take a devastating hit.

This book is written to help you promote positive thinking, joy, and happiness. I want to transform the relationship between your work and life by utilizing the powerful human ability to create meaning. You can achieve success in any situation and any circumstance. Success happens with clear intentions, engagement, strategies, and focus. What makes you happy and successful? Although the combination is elusive, you can be both happy and successful.

As a philosophy major in college, I enjoyed exploring the thought process behind philosophical

INTRODUCTION

ideas. Some of these concepts are relevant and empowering to me even now. You can adopt some of these ideas to expand your knowledge and develop new ideas. Moreover, you get to choose which philosophies work to your advantage. This book will examine some relevant philosophical theories you can adapt to expand your viewpoints. Since life is a journey, consider that each chapter takes you to a new place where you can explore and grow.

This book has two types of suggestions: tools and systemic interventions. You can pick up the tools when needed and then leave them on the shelf for another day. Systemic interventions are part of ongoing efforts to change how you live or work. They require regular engagement as a part of your way of living.

In the first part of the book, Reinventing You, you will explore your situation and who you are. This understanding invites you to be more aware and become the best version of yourself. By connecting with others meaningfully, you can develop a reliable support system to overcome challenges, increase well-being, and decrease health risks. In the second part, Finding the Work You Want, you will figure out why you are working and create meaning for your work. The third part, Tools and Skills for Sustainability, offers practical help to overcome internal stressors so you can see more options and possibilities. The final part, the Ultimate Human Goal, deeply explores the concept of happiness and offers habits to make yourself happier. Since finding happiness and success begins by looking inside yourself, the journey will not be easy, but once you find your way, it will all be worth it.

# Part I

# Reinventing You

Become the best version of yourself. Who are you? If you are not completely sure, this book is written for you. By the end of this part, you will be able to confidently answer who you are, who you want to be, and how to create the meaning you want in your life.

In this part, we will cover how essential it is to have clear intentions, how to choose what actions to prioritize out of all the potential things to do, and how to focus your energy and attention. Selecting the values and the principles you live by helps you make commitments and have direction. They will help you to be successful and be your authentic self. Your values will change as you take up new roles. Sometimes you may shift your priorities. However, remember that you can still be true to yourself and who you want to become, even as you change.

What connections do you have with your loved ones and others? How resilient are you? Together, we'll explore these questions and how they can help you find happiness and success.

# CHAPTER 1

# Where Are You Now?

*The purpose of life is not to be happy. It is to be useful, to be honorable, to be compassionate, to have it make some difference that you have lived and lived well.*
—Ralph Waldo Emerson

Do you know where you are now and where you are headed? How would you describe your current self, your current situation, and your current assets? I do not mean your financial assets but your abilities and capacities. Before you get to the new future of possibilities, you should understand the current state in realistic terms.

According to the American Psychological Association Trends Report, "Burnout and stress are at all-time highs across all professions . . . American workers across the board saw heightened burnout in 2021. . . . 79 percent of employees had experienced work-related stress the month before" (Abramson 2022). The World Health Organization defines burnout

HAPPY SUCCESSFUL YOU

*Am I experiencing total burnout?*

as a syndrome resulting from workplace stress that has not been managed. These dimensions characterize it: feelings of energy depletion or exhaustion, increased mental distance from one's job, feelings of cynicism or negativism related to one's job, and reduced professional efficacy (Turner 2019).

## Assess Where You Are

What is your situation? Will your situation improve, or is it getting worse? Are you experiencing burnout or stress? Are you feeling stuck? Those suffering from burnout are frequently overwhelmed, emotionally exhausted, unfeeling, cynical, impersonal, disengaged, and ineffective. The most important thing is recognizing burnout when it happens to you or someone close to you.

For a burnout assessment, consider the following questions:

- Do you feel overwhelmed or helpless?
- Do you lack the energy to complete tasks?
- Is it difficult for you to concentrate?
- Do you feel numb or disengaged from others?
- Have you become cynical or irritable?
- Do you feel that you are ineffective?

If you say yes to several of these questions, you may be experiencing burnout.

Chronic stress that causes burnout comes from having little or no control over the outcome of events and how they're handled. Faced with such situations, you find it hard to get motivated. Burnout is the equivalent of your mind and body throwing their hands up and saying, "I can't." The longer this condition persists, the higher the chance of developing mental issues, such as depression or substance abuse, which require professional help.

Let us start with what is going well. What areas in your work are satisfying? Are there people you work with who support you? What aspects of your job do you control? What do you enjoy about your work?

What parts of your personal life are you happy with? Who supports you in your personal life? Do you have ways to strengthen your connections or your relationship with others?

For those of you feeling stuck and needing help to see options or possibilities, the next section will help you. You can develop new ways of viewing your situation and solving challenges using creativity.

Assessing your current situation is difficult because you are so immersed in it. You may need to get out of yourself to see your blind spots. I will help you figure out different ways of viewing your life.

## New Possibilities

Let us invite some new views to help you recognize opportunities in life or work. How can you look for new possibilities or adopt different outlooks? I am introducing the four *R*s: refocus, reperspective, reframe, and reevaluate. They are tools to look at things differently. Tools are available when needed and can be put away until the next time you need them. Initially, you'll use these tools frequently to build daily or weekly habits.

## *Refocus*

As an ophthalmologist, I perform many of my surgeries under a microscope. When I supervise residents, teaching starts with the microscope. One of the first difficulties for our trainees is finding the appropriate magnification and proper focus to perform surgeries. You get a much more extensive view of the area at low magnification. However, as you magnify, the view area gets smaller and more sensitive to proper focus, so the effect of a slight change in direction also gets magnified.

> **When you get hyperfocused on small details, you will miss the big picture and miss out on much of life.**

Life works in similar ways. When you get hyperfocused on small details, you will miss the big picture and miss out on much of life. You may miss obvious opportunities right in front of you. If you are not in proper focus, even a routine task can have the possibility of errors. Distractions can interrupt your concentration and focus.

For example, when I do a surgery and the patient moves just a bit, it looks like an earthquake under the microscope. In response, the first thing to do is to decrease the magnification to find the bigger picture to ensure the patient's movement did not cause any problems. If there are problems, I will assess what I need to fix.

Sometimes I do need to work under higher magnification for delicate work. Focusing on the different levels of the lens in the eye is essential. For example, during cataract surgery, I need to make an opening in the front of the lens to access the inside of the lens. As I continue to work on the lens, I need to carefully remove the center of the lens without disturbing the back part of the lens capsule, which is about five to seven microns thick. (A human hair is about seventy microns wide.) This is where I place the lens implant inside this natural lens capsule. As magnification increases, more precise focus is necessary for optimal visualization and accuracy. Determining precisely what you want to do during each moment is critical. It takes practice to make sure your movements are small under the microscope.

In life, the proper magnification and focus are necessary. As you become sensitive to where you are, remember that your field of vision is tiny in higher magnification. Occasionally, seeing things at a lower magnification is essential to get the overall picture and to remind you why you are there in the first place.

Consider your life as though you are looking through a microscope and realize where you are focused and what you are trying to do. This close, careful view can be daunting and takes practice, but it is essential to creating what you want to see happen. With practice, you can master this way of viewing life. Are you living your life with purpose and happiness? How would it be different if you believed you could have meaning and happiness? What are the things in your work that you have control over? What are the goals you would like to accomplish? What have you learned about what you need to do to succeed? Come up with your standards, and do not compare yourself to others.

Focusing on the things you can control and reflecting on your past experiences and achievements provide energy and renewal. Concentrating on what you can control allows you to beam your energy to things you can improve rather than squandering it. It is inefficient and unhealthy to focus on the things you have no power over—all it does is make you feel powerless.

## *Reperspective*

Instead of constantly looking from your perspective, consider other viewpoints. What would the bigger picture look like from someone else's eyes? Will this matter in a month or a year? What biases do you have that you may not be able to recognize? How could you construct views that include all the perspectives?

For example, your boss could be concerned with adding a new service line and increasing productivity in health care. If your boss wants to add a new service line, it may mean adding a new machine or new learning for the physician and staff through additional training. Of course, it helps when the boss uses an outstanding approach and the right motivation. The employees are generally happy to do what they are asked to do. The boss may also be considering the patients' point of view; they want quality health care at a reasonable cost with excellent service. If you thought of all these viewpoints simultaneously, you could create an outlook encompassing all bosses, physicians, staff, patients, and even insurance. This is the multiview perspective, which can be refined when gathering more information.

When was the last time you considered your boss's point of view? What is it that your boss would like from you and why? When was the most recent frank conversation with your boss? What do your coworkers expect from you and why? Are these expectations in line with your goals and values?

By considering other people's perspectives, you can appreciate different ways of thinking and feeling. Your possible actions may change when you sense others' perspectives. As a physician, I challenge myself frequently to think from a patient's perspective. It has helped me relate to patients more efficiently and explain ideas to them. For example, I have assured patients that by using numbing eye drops, they will have no pain, which is a significant concern patients always have.

Another example outside of work illustrates how our perspectives influence and limit us.

A mom asks her daughter, "What kind of pizza would you like?"

Her daughter answers, "Pepperoni pizza, please!"

The mom ordered a pepperoni pizza and a supreme pizza for herself. Then the mom asked, "Are you sure you do not want a slice of the supreme pizza?"

"No, Mom," the daughter answers, frustrated. "You never listen to what I say."

Because the mom grew up in a large family where she often felt left out, she always wanted to ensure everyone around her felt included. As a mom, she overdoes things and wonders if her daughter may have changed her mind. Meanwhile, the daughter wanted her preferences to be respected and translated the question to mean her mom never remembered or respected her opinions.

Imagine if both considered each other's point of view. That misunderstanding would quickly become history.

Step back from your point of view and your interpretations of your situation and consider other viewpoints. What opportunities are open for you now?

Why is this important? You may think you need more options or choices when you feel stuck. Therefore, it is vital to consider some other points of view to give you new insights.

## *Reframe*

Reframing is a way to look at something in a different context; sometimes, it could be simply getting to the issue without any judgmental language. In that case, looking at just the facts will help. For example, the technicians who check in with the patient will sometimes notice that the patient is belligerent or angry. I ask what exactly happened that gave them that impression. If there are any negative notes or thinking patterns, ask yourself what it could look like if you delete those negative thoughts. What would it look like if you replaced them with more positive ones? Negativity could be your own interpretation of the situation.

How can you look at situations differently? Do you see the world in extremes, in black and white? Our world has many shades of gray and silver. These colors can look similar, except that we associate silver more positively than gray because of the shiny, metallic tone. In contrast, the grays are flat and not as exciting. When you get into this all-or-nothing mode, recognize that and think of all the beautiful silver tones. How did those thoughts translate to your feelings and emotions? Do you feel more positive and more confident about yourself?

Reframing takes practice. You can change your thoughts from being overwhelmed by paperwork to viewing the task in more easy or doable pieces. This calms your anxious thoughts and feelings and makes a world of difference. Taking a pause and breathing deeply can help.

How about a situation where you are driving and notice more cars than usual? Are your first thoughts negative? Assuming you are not in a hurry, could you consider it positively, such as time for music or more alone time, instead of tensing up with stress? Your thoughts and emotions together create your actions.

For example, if you are excited about a new software update because you believe that the update can solve the problem you have been having, such as typing all descriptions instead of choosing from options, then your emotions would be more positive, which can create positive actions. Whereas if you dread coming to work because of the software upgrades and believe that this software upgrade will slow you down, your emotions will be more anxious and worried. Although any new learning can take time, if you are willing to take the time now for benefits in the future, you can gain positivity in your view. On top of that, you generally look to others to confirm what you believe in, so you will look for your allies: coworkers with similar viewpoints.

Your thoughts, feelings, and emotions color your views and affect your actions. Recognizing your current thoughts and feelings is the first step. Then, imagine if you choose to adjust or change any of those thoughts and emotions to change your course of action before it happens. It can be powerful.

## *Reevaluate*

When you cannot help but dwell on your shortcomings, reflecting on your positive accomplishments will help build self-confidence and awareness. That self-awareness will help you apply yourself optimally. For this to work well, you might need a way to record all your achievements. A habit tracker app can help, such as Productive Habit Tracker, Habit Tracker, or Fabulous, to name a few. Alternatively, you can record them in a diary or journal and look at them for inspiration.

To get started, write down achievements you are proud of. They can be achievements in your life or your job. They can be personal milestones, like losing weight, running five miles regularly, or your ability to focus for a certain number of hours. Some achievements will be formal, like getting a qualification or an award.

This practice produces a sense of direction. When you do this, you start to form a powerful narrative of yourself and where you are headed. What stories are you telling yourself? Are you looking at all this with a positive lens or at least a neutral, realistic lens? Do not ruminate on negative views, which can lead to a downward spiral.

Once you have that list, keep it somewhere easily accessible. If your office is private, you can put it up somewhere in your view as a constant reminder of what you have accomplished. Try pinning a note on your desktop and look at it for inspiration.

By utilizing all four *Rs*—refocus, reperspective, reframe, and reevaluate—you will be open to new possibilities and opportunities. These tools help you to look at your thoughts and emotions differently to create different actions. How can you expect different outcomes if you always have similar thoughts and feelings? It is essential to realize that having more positive thoughts, insights, and emotions is a good starting point, but it's not enough. Creating action plans based on those thoughts and feelings sustains your changes.

## Time Is Limited

Our time is limited. Although this may be a grim way of thinking about life, it is very effective. Considering your limited time, you sense urgency and can realize your priorities, direction, and motivation.

Time is precious. If there is no tomorrow, how would you prioritize your day? What would be the most important thing for you right now? You can only live in the moment. Would you find your loved ones and spend more time with them, or would you go see a place on your bucket list? What would you do?

During the recent COVID pandemic, many faced our mortality and considered what matters in life. It helped us think about our values and the principles that we uphold in our lives. Most of us knew someone who had passed due to COVID. Some of us considered quality versus quantity in relationships. In addition to using video chat/conference platforms like Zoom to work remotely, we started using them to connect with friends and family we could not see in person.

Awareness of mortality can teach us many things. Although death is an unavoidable part of the cycle of life, we try to do everything we can to avoid death. As a medical student on the oncology floor, I saw that most people wanted to live longer by any means possible, even if it meant risking side effects and complications that would keep them in the hospital. However, what struck me was the few individuals who cherished the life given to them. If you can accept that your life will be over, it can also enable you to cherish every moment.

Despite the strong labor demand, the Great Resignation began in the spring of 2021 when US workers started resigning at an elevated rate. This trend continued through 2022. This resulted in staff shortages, especially among those in service industries like nursing, retail, and restaurants. The Great Resignation resulted from necessary questions of what people want as workers and human beings.

At the same time, the quiet resignation is also happening. Quiet quitting is when workers do the bare necessities to keep their jobs but are no longer fully invested (Newport 2022). They may still be working next to you. It may have been a response to burnout, exhaustion, or a toxic culture without signs of change. These factors make people feel that their work life could be more satisfactory. If many people are quiet quitting, will there be any innovation, discovery, or progress?

The same feelings and patterns can happen in your personal life. Do you feel like you are in a rut? Are you doing the same thing repeatedly and hoping for a different outcome? If your process is the same, then how can the outcome differ? How can we change the process for a better outcome?

Living in a fast-paced world and being blocked by the pandemic made many people realize they had to deal with the unexpected. Many of us felt like we had no choices, that the events around us were inevitable, and that our efforts made no difference. Physicians or other frontline workers had to go to work through the pandemic, but most people had to work from home and juggle not having reliable daycare and schools for kids and many changes outside their control. Some of us gained flexibility, agility, adaptability, and more understanding of others.

Your life is getting more complicated, uncertain, and even accelerating now that the height of the pandemic is over. During the pandemic, we had an excuse for not living a "normal" life. We faulted everything due to the pandemic. We had travel restrictions, limited direct contact with people, and changes in our active lifestyles. Due to the pandemic, I still have not returned to the gym or crowded indoor spaces, like movies, symphonies, and plays. Of course, people who enjoyed the outdoors, such as golf, may have increased those activities.

The world has changed business as usual, but it will never return to how it was. COVID is still with us and changing, and many people are not considering how to protect themselves. Most of us are still figuring out how to navigate the still-evolving changes in the world.

None of us know how much time we have. How would you like to spend your limited time now?

How do you prioritize what is essential? What are you able to do right now? Your most valuable and scarce resources are time and attention. Are you living a meaningful life now, and how do you make a difference? These questions may feel heavy, but they can motivate you toward your desired successful, happy life.

## What Made Your Life Meaningful?

First, realize that the past is the past. We cannot change the past. Of course, you may try to make amends in some cases, but you still cannot go back to the past. Looking at your life now, what is most meaningful to you?

- What gives you meaning in your life?
- What makes sense for your priorities? What makes your life worth living?
- When do you feel most alive?
- If you imagine yourself at the end of your life, what are you most proud of?
- What made your life extraordinary?

Write down some of the answers that come to you.

- Reflect on your strengths and when you use them most. What experiences come to mind?
- What are your life's positive and enriching experiences? Remember when you made a difference in someone else's life or something important to you went well.
- What about you or how you acted made things go well?
- What gifts, talents, or strengths did you bring to the situation?
- What effects did you create for yourself and others?

As an ophthalmologist, I've helped patients see the best they could. In addition, I want their eyes to feel as comfortable as possible. We take everything for granted until our eyes hurt or make us unable to see. When patients improve their sight, such as after cataract surgeries, I have noticed that their beliefs, perspectives, and mindsets improve. For example, I had a patient who returned to work after a long retirement when he realized his renewed abilities.

As an executive coach, I help my clients to expand their beliefs, perspectives, and mindsets. This is not by changing their physical vision but by challenging and supporting clients to think differently. This has created new innovative thoughts and other creative actions.

To find your strengths, consider what comes naturally to you or the proudest moments in your journey. What roles or activities brought you vitality? When someone compliments you, what do they mention about you? This reflection will give you more confidence and awareness.

Where do you want to invest your attention? For example, as I write this book for you, I must be aware, focused, attentive, and fully present to achieve my ultimate performance. When fully present, I will be completely immersed in the activity and free from distractions or interference. This requires me to be completely cognizant of my current resources, capabilities, and conscious thoughts.

Here is an easy technique. Pause, take a few deep breaths, and be fully present. Thinking about the moment you are in can feel awkward initially, but fully appreciating it as it occurs helps you understand the moment and creates your ultimate control. For example, feel the chair you are sitting on. Feel the back of the chair and be fully present. Listen to any sounds around you. Feel the warmth or coolness of the air around you. Look at what is right in front of you. Are there any scents in the air?

If you want to take the next step, the best way is to be fully present in the moment you are in now, not the past or the future. Set aside any worries or negative thoughts. Bad memories come from when we are distracted, not fully present, and not focused on the moment.

> **If you want to take the next step, the best way is to be fully present in the moment you are in now, not the past or the future.**

In this chapter, you started with the current stage of your life and learned to refocus, reperspective, reframe, and reevaluate to gain new insights and opportunities. In the next chapter, you get to choose to invest in yourself. Develop your strengths, talents, and skills to their maximum potential. This will require a lot of practice and time, but choosing yourself is a decisive step to creating meaning and purpose.

**CHAPTER 2**

# Choosing You

*Life has no meaning a priori . . . It is up to you to give it a meaning, and value is nothing but the meaning that you choose.*
— Jean-Paul Sartre

How much time do you invest in becoming the best of your abilities? Are you struggling in your job or wanting to get better at something? How much time and energy will you spend on that one thing for yourself? You can't wait to become less busy or until someone else helps you. No one can invest in you except you. Know yourself and determine where you stand or how to measure it objectively.

Of course, remember that one thing you are interested in will change as your priorities change. If you intentionally choose yourself and strategically plan to improve, it is very possible that you will one day be all you aim to be. Remember to choose just one thing instead of several things. Practice every day and commit.

HAPPY SUCCESSFUL YOU

*I am choosing to develop my full potential!*

For example, when the first laser became available in 1995, I wanted to learn new skills in refractive surgery, like laser vision corrections, such as PRK (photorefractive keratectomy) and LASIK (laser-assisted in situ keratomileusis). Learning new skills takes time and dedication. I read, watched videos, and thought about it whenever I could. I attended meetings and learned more. After the laser certification, I visited other experts and learned more about what to do and what not to do. After I mastered it, what I wanted to learn changed. Now I am learning golf and would love to get better.

Existential philosophers, including Søren Kierkegaard, Friedrich Nietzsche, Jean-Paul Sartre, and Simone de Beauvoir, framed existentialism as seeking meaning in life (Bamford 2019). I was drawn to existentialism because it concerns ways to explain individual human experiences in a universe we do not understand.

"Experiencing meaning in life is important to well-being and health" (Martela 2016). Researchers have a few ways to understand what meaning is in life: coherence, purpose, and significance. Coherence means a sense of comprehensibility and one's life making sense. Purpose means a sense of life's goals, aims, and direction. The third, now gaining attention, is significance, the importance of life's inherent value and that life is worth living. I use *meaning* loosely in this book to mean all three items: coherence, purpose, and significance.

## Using Philosophical Ideas to Create Meaning

Existentialists believe that individuals exist as free and responsible agents who determine their acts of will. It is the philosophical belief that we are each responsible for creating purpose and meaning in our lives. Because we are entirely free and the universe does not make sense, we cannot derive our purpose and meaning from others, such as gods, governments, teachers, or other authorities (Bakewell 2016). Existentialism was not limited to philosophers, as many writers, such as Fyodor Dostoevsky, Franz Kafka, and Samuel Beckett, explored its ideas as a cultural movement.

Existentialism proposes that existence precedes essence; we are, first and foremost, independent conscious beings. For Sartre, "We mean that man first of all exists, encounters himself, surges up in the world—and defines himself afterward" (Sartre 1946). Since humanity is not born with any predetermined purpose, we create ourselves. Therefore, life is full of choices, and you can make your own choices, including seeking meaning in life, examining meaning in your own way, and responding to human existence. Sartre also said, "Life is C between B and D," *choice* between *birth* and *death*. He was a firm believer that you are responsible for your choices.

Albert Camus supported the philosophy of absurdism; he thought that life is senseless, purposeless, and meaningless (Camus 1955). Camus acknowledges the tension between human's desire for order, meaning, and happiness and the indifferent natural universe that creates a sense of incomprehensible contradiction or the absurd. The key to understanding Camus is that this realization of the absurd is not the end but the beginning. This beginning allows you to rebel against the absurd by exercising freedom and living the present life fully. He asserts that rebels will embrace life for life's sake, make new connections with the rest of humanity, and live passionately.

On the other hand, earlier in the nineteenth century, Søren Kierkegaard, known as the father of existentialism, rejected reason in the battle against absurdity. His solution involved a "leap of faith." In other words, since faith does not have reason, logic, or rationality, he allows that believing in God would require a leap of faith. This may not be easy to accept for some existentialists who may not believe in God (McDonald 2023).

Not all existentialists come to the same conclusions. That is the beauty of philosophy. In evaluating a philosophical argument, the importance is not the conclusion. If the premises are accurate and the idea succeeds logically, the value is in thinking through the argument. Again, the value is in the process, not the outcome.

What makes life meaningful is a vast question, and many different theoretical approaches exist. For example, could meaningful lives be meaningful by participating in a larger view than an individual's welfare or advantage? This view is called self-transcendence.

Although there is no explicit, precise characterization of what is meaningful in life, there is a common strand in all the theories, philosophies, and religions. This common belief is that we can consider our lives unique and meaningful. This belief is essential because having a meaningful life has higher positive effects, like satisfaction, fulfillment, and resilience in stressful situations.

Your life's meaning may have all three components —coherence, purpose, and significance—but not necessarily all of them at all times. What would the result look like if you searched for your meaning? Defining your terminology determines the outcome. What do you consider meaningful? For example, if you imagine someone who sets the bar too high for purpose, they quickly fail to find meaning and significance. Therefore, Landau discusses that it is up to the individual to seek the appropriate meaning in life. Sometimes we must attune ourselves to enhance and appreciate importance. The pursuit of our goals itself can give a sense of purpose (Landau 2017).

Existentialism allows you to have the freedom to define your meaning. You get to decide what and how to dedicate your life. Recognize that you are not constrained by anything in the past. Look at the future from your present viewpoint, and use your will to decide what your life will be like going forward. You create your future by making choices. I have taken this stance since it is straightforward, meaningful, and applicable to most people. This idea helps people clarify and choose among different lifestyles to create more prosperous and meaningful lives.

You can live a life you choose, as unique as you are. Looking at this as a huge opportunity, you will realize that you do not need to follow what others have prescribed. What I find most empowering about existentialism is that you are responsible for creating your purpose and meaning in your life. This idea empowers you!

Many people feel they have meaningful professions that help others, such as doctors, lawyers, and religious leaders. Other people derive meaning from volunteer work, travel, or creating music or art. If you value those activities, you are indeed creating value for yourself.

Creating happiness is based on learning what makes you feel good and happy, like visiting a new place, discovering your abilities, accomplishing new projects, or simply finishing your work on time. It could be a clever idea or anything that gives you joy, satisfaction, and fulfillment.

## Develop Your Potential

Choosing you means that you are placing yourself as a priority, developing yourself to your full potential, and being authentic so that you will live as the best version of yourself. It also requires you to accept yourself as a whole unit. Choosing yourself is living an intentional life with a message to yourself about what you plan to do. Intentional choices mean you are choosing to do one thing instead of another. You are saying no to everything else.

> **Intentional choices mean you are choosing to do one thing instead of another. You are saying no to everything else.**

First, you invest in yourself to determine your desires. Let's take time to dream of living your chosen life. What would that look like to you?

- What are you doing?
- What are you thinking and feeling?

- Where is your attention?
- Where are you?
- Who are you with?

You can create the steps toward that direction by articulating what you want. Write down what life choices you would choose. Write the thoughts that arise.

Now look at your present life. Are you listening to yourself, your needs, and your desires? Do you know what you want or what outcome you are hoping for? What direction are you headed? If you cannot articulate what you want, how do you expect those things to appear magically? How would you know once you have achieved it? How do you achieve success when you cannot even recognize it? What do you mean by success? How do you want the success to look, feel, sound, taste, and smell?

Use your focus and concentration to be intentional. Remember to choose your options based on your needs and desires instead of the influences of others, such as family, friends, and society, which may result in conflicts, despair, unhappiness, and powerlessness.

None of us are born with all the talents, skills, and insights we need for success. Most of us need to figure out where we are and develop many of the necessary talents and skills, including formal education in some cases. Feel free to learn, even if you are older and seem to learn more slowly than before. Create a growth plan to reach your maximum potential and accept that you constantly change. With intention, that change will be for the better.

When I was in high school, I thought that playing piano created joy for me and others. I practiced and practiced until some of my family complained that I was being too loud since the piano was in the living room and the house was small. Playing the piano meant that I could be transported to another place to explore all the emotions in the music. I thought that would be the gift I wanted to share. For me, it was a way to show my emotions of love, anger, boredom, grief, and sadness. I was crushed when my parents told me I was not meant to be a pianist and stopped my lessons! My parents thought playing piano should be a hobby, not a profession. As a struggling immigrant family, they thought a profession must allow financial freedom.

In retrospect, thanks to all my piano practices, I became a perfectionist and a high achiever. When I decided to become a surgeon in medical school and looked for different surgical specialties, I knew that playing piano had led me to become an ophthalmologist. Although I did not become a pianist, I realized ophthalmic surgeries are delicate, precise, and demanding, like a piano performance. The music was precise, especially the technical parts. I had to be exact, just like eye surgeries. In the operating room, I focus on giving my best performance, allowing me to be my best self.

When choosing the path you want to use to create meaning, you must understand how to create and sustain a presence. The past is something to learn from and the future is unpredictable, so your only time is now. You can only focus on one activity at a time. This allows you to operate in each moment with your full senses and intuition to guide you from one moment to the next.

The feeling of control happens when you are in the moment, not the past or future. Feeling out of control is stressful. Of course, many things can distract you from the present moment, such as revisiting previous meetings or conversations in your mind. If you need to take a few minutes to reconsider the last moments, then do so; that's introspection or self-reflection. However, you are not fully present when you are doing that.

From my high school days of wanting to be a pianist, I moved on to attend the honors college at the University of Michigan. It was the only school I applied to since my parents did not want to pay for other application fees, and it was an in-state school for my family. My parents wanted a physician in the family, and they were determined that I was it. During my college years, however, I pursued a double major in philosophy, which I enjoyed. In addition, I majored in cellular and molecular biology to take all the required premed classes.

Since my parents worked so hard for the family in the US, I did not want to disappoint them. I worked hard too. One thing that I realized afterward is that it is not my job to make my parents happy. It is theirs.

According to my parents, attending the University of Michigan Medical School was my natural progression, and again, I only applied to one school. I also got into the Medical Scientist Training Program (MSTP). It is a training program funded by the National Institutes of Health (NIH) for physician-scientists to receive both degrees of MD and PhD, and the program covers everything, including tuition, books, and fees, including living stipends. I applied to this prestigious program not because I wanted a PhD but because it would help me with the finances. I worked hard, although it was not my first choice. Medicine was what my parents wanted me to do. What I wanted to do was to attend law school since many of my philosophy friends were attending law school. However, I did not want my parents to be disappointed in me, and I did not have the guts to fight them. I wanted to do well enough to get into a residency program of my choice to further my career. At that time, the program was what I was meant to do, so I worked hard.

Honestly, I did not have any role models. No one in my family or anyone close to me was a physician. My life took another turn when I decided to drop the MSTP. Staying an extra three years for the PhD would be an ordeal when I did not enjoy the medical school years. Instead, I applied to be a Howard Hughes Medical Institute-NIH research scholar. I took a year off from medical school to research at NIH in Bethesda, Maryland. I met my husband that year. I got married during my last year in medical school, and I had another person's viewpoint to consider.

Being an intern was challenging, and on top of that, I became pregnant during my internship. Yes, life happens! Initially, I could hide my pregnancy for four to five months. I did not know how to tell the people around me, from the program director to my coworkers. I did not know what to ask myself because I was trying to survive. I wish I had asked myself: How resilient are you? But you may only know the answer once you go through the experience. Being yourself should be effortless, except when you are a pregnant intern with no maternity leave. I had to save my vacation and sick days to get four weeks off the internship for the delivery of my first child. That was my maternity leave.

We all have different interests, talents, strengths, and life situations. Under the circumstances, we make our own choices. However, developing our potential to the fullest whenever possible is important. You may not realize what opportunity will show up. When we are young and inexperienced, our biggest influencers are our parents and guardians.

## Develop Your Strengths

Intuition tells us to work on our weaknesses. You may not think of your strengths as things to be improved. Strengths are not just what you are good at, and weaknesses aren't what you are bad at; those definitions are too simplistic. Strengths are things that can energize and engage you (Buckingham 2007). Ask yourself what kinds of activities excite, stimulate, and encourage you. They are your true strengths.

Strengths make you feel successful and confident and even engender a flow state (Greene 2019). Positive psychologist Mihaly Csikszentmihalyi first described the flow state. Flow is the mental state where we are so immersed in a feeling of energized focus, full involvement, and enjoyment of the activity that we lose the sense of space and time. When you develop your strengths, it will make you much happier.

> **Your strengths can constantly be improved, expanded, or used in novel ways.**

Using your strengths more at work makes you happier and helps you experience less stress, feel healthier, have more energy, and be engaged and confident. You may feel more creative, satisfied, and experience more meaning in your work (McQuaid 2014).

Your strengths can constantly be improved, expanded, or used in novel ways. That is what developing them is all about. To do that, you need to know what your strengths are. Knowing your strengths comes from thinking, noticing, listening, and asking. Write your strengths down.

*Think* back to activities that you enjoy doing. These should come quickly. Ask yourself what skills or qualities you use when you do them. Those are your strengths. For instance, working with data might be your strength if you lose track of time when analyzing information. If time flies when you write editorials, your strengths could be writing, communication, and journalism. I used to sit at the piano for more than three hours, practicing until someone interrupted me.

*Notice* what sorts of things others approach you with for help or ideas. If people keep coming to you when their computer malfunctions, you may be good at technology. You might take that for granted and not think it is a big deal, but you overlook it precisely because it is a strength. You might be upset that your friends only come when their relationships are in shambles, but maybe that is because you are good at listening or helping people with interpersonal problems.

*Listen* to people when they compliment you. A criticism can reveal your weaknesses, but a compliment highlights a strength. Think back to the feedback you have received. People congratulated me, "That was a great presentation you gave." That helped me realize that communication and public speaking are my strengths. If someone says, "You never know when to let things go." It is a criticism that also reveals a strength: you are tenacious. That can be improved and used the right way. Listen carefully to what people say to you.

*Ask* people who know you well, like family, colleagues, or friends, what they think your strengths are. Not all people will be helpful, but you can't learn if you do not ask. You could also take an online assessment to figure out your strengths. There are assessments such as StrengthsFinder, CliftonStrengths, or DiSC. I asked some of my colleagues what my strengths are. The response that surprised me most was, "You are so diplomatic! How do you say no to someone with a smile?" In our hospital meetings, even when they were contentious, I acknowledged and validated people's feelings before I said what was on my mind without apology or hesitation. From there, I was open to negotiating and compromising.

Once you know your strengths, you can start improving them, starting with what most interests you. You can improve them by learning a related skill, taking a class, or using them more often. Feel free to experiment with your strengths.

## Dimensions of Self

What are the dimensions of yourself? Why is this important? You cannot be successful if you cannot accept all of yourself—your physical, mental, emotional, spiritual, and social selves. Being aware of and understanding all these dimensions is integral to choosing you. Accepting your whole self will help you grow and not work against yourself.

When you are feeling physically, mentally, emotionally, spiritually, and socially solid and active, you have the best chance of experiencing all the energy and vitality you need to complete the tasks and goals that are important to you. Let us analyze each dimension separately to see how it influences you and how to utilize them for your benefit.

*Physical* areas include general health, nutrition, sleep, exercise, body image, injury, and illnesses. These areas can be divided further to optimize each subsection to operate at its highest potential. Health is an essential part of your well-being and part of the journey of life. We are all born with potential, but we can develop it to be our best. Remember that enough sleep, for example, varies widely from person to person. The goal is full functionality or functioning best for your desired individual experiences.

For example, I had an opportunity to attend the wedding of a good friend who has paraplegia.

He married a nurse he had known well during his extended hospital stay. He had great spirits and had studied to be a social worker to assist others in similar situations. He looked handsome in his black tuxedo in his wheelchair with a ramp over the stairs at the altar. On the dance floor at the reception afterward, he did wheelies in the wheelchair, and his physical state did not limit his fun. He had to express his dancing differently, but the audience could share his joy and excitement about the event.

*Mental* or brain power is another dimension, including alertness, clarity, concentration, focus, memory, and creativity. Finding the optimal levels of alertness can depend on the time of the day. Are you a morning person or a night owl? Do you experience a four o'clock slump? Remember that these will vary between individuals and may be affected by caffeine consumption and other factors. Figuring out when your brain functions best can help you to achieve success and happiness.

Focus is what you pay attention to, and concentration is maintaining your attention. For example, imagine that you are a golfer. What are you focusing on? Is it the spots where you want your ball to be on the green or the bunker you want to avoid? Concentrate on what you want provides a more precise direction than what you try to avoid.

As with a microscope, your focus can be narrow or broad. For example, while writing this book, I sometimes narrow my focus to expressing my thoughts in words. Whereas, if I am speaking about this book, I may keep my focus broader to notice my audience's reactions to what I am saying.

I learned that envisioning my piano recitals going smoothly helped me before the event. I imagined playing the whole piece in my mind. I created the outcome I wanted to see for myself. The more details you put into this mental imagery practice, the better. I would start near the piano, where I would announce my piece, and then I would sit at the piano. Just looking at my music without playing the work can create the music in my mind. I could hear the music in my mind with all accurate notes and musical expressions. I even bowed at the end.

To develop your mental strength, seek mindfulness, centering, and meditation activities. As a result, you will improve your concentration, which will help you relax and become calmer and more peaceful in all your actions.

*Emotional* areas are how you think about, express, and manage emotions. Emotions are instinctive or intuitive states of feelings distinguished from reasoning or knowledge, and they derive from one's circumstances, mood, or relationships with others. We often misunderstand our emotions. As a result, we tend to react instead of looking at the purpose of the feeling. When you face emotion, try to figure out what the emotion is trying to tell you. Emotion is a valuable tool to help you understand what you're experiencing.

If someone does not show emotions, do you find them cold, unapproachable, or apathetic? Are you expressing some feelings inappropriately? For example, do you storm out of the room or roll your eyes when disagreeing? It is okay to say that you agree to disagree.

The goal is to understand your emotions and others' emotions to express your feelings appropriately. Remember that your beliefs, attitudes, and thoughts help create your emotions. There are a few different theories of how emotions are formed, but that is beyond the scope of this book.

I grew up in a household where my family rarely showed emotions or discussed how we felt. It seemed that emotion was not important. My parents rarely showed their emotions. Some cultures or people believe that showing your emotions is a sign of weakness. I was encouraged to share what I thought of things and actions I had taken, but I was rarely asked how I felt.

Now, I feel free to share my feelings and emotions, as I have learned that particular emotions are not associated with judgment. Withhold any judgment, like good or bad, right or wrong, or positive or negative. Instead, accept emotions as signals in your body for you to understand and create actions that can guide you. Although it was not easy initially, I felt more alive as I got better at sharing my emotions. I was pleasantly surprised at how others reacted to me. They accepted me as I was, and no one questioned me.

Experts suggest there are five to seven basic emotions. They are anger, fear, sadness, disgust, happiness, surprise, and guilt. Here I am discussing the most common five emotions. Our ability to combine and mix emotions with various intensities can complicate how we feel.

- Anger is the belief that there is a threat to yourself or someone or something that you love. Anger is a perception of certainty and individual control, so anger can increase risk-taking behavior. Anger can come up when protecting others, and the threat may not involve you directly. On the surface, anger and fear can appear similar, but examining further, you will notice the difference.
- Fear is born out of self-protection. Fear keeps you alive by protecting you from actual or perceived danger or potentially losing what you value. Fear is more of the perception of uncertainty and situational control. Fear generally refers to our own self-protection, and fear is less likely to lead to risk-taking behaviors (Habib 2015).
- Happiness is a pleasant emotional state with contentment, joy, and satisfaction.

- Guilt has a lot to do with how what you do differs from who you want to be. You feel guilty when you say or go against the person you want to be or think you should be.
- Sadness and grief occur when you lose someone or something, including a dream or hope. Sadness can show up as a disappointment in yourself, others, or a situation. It reminds you of the gifts of life that you have lost.

Emotions are powerful if you can face them. They can feel life-changing or even profound at times. Looking at the big picture, like your purpose or values, what is essential to you and why? Instead of feeling bad when you have emotions that seem bad or negative, like sadness, grief, and guilt, figure out what it is trying to tell you. To control your emotions is to respond to them thoughtfully and not just react to them. Your reaction may have your interpretation of what is happening. Unfortunately, many people misunderstand emotions and only react to them. They end up living with the effects of their emotions. Emotions only hold the power you give them.

Think of a recent situation in which a strong feeling came up. Ask the following questions to yourself. What were you feeling? What was the feeling telling you about how you were interpreting what was happening? What in this situation was causing you to feel this way?

What thoughts were underlying your emotions? Were there any physical sensations? What actions did these feelings make you take? Become a detective and check in with yourself. Building emotional intelligence means learning to manage your emotions by responding to your own feelings and others'. Remember to pause to respond instead of reacting.

To go even deeper, learn to figure out what triggers certain emotions. Are there any patterns of what triggers your certain emotions? If you often feel disappointed or sad because your expectations are unmet, it would be best to let go of the outcome, realizing it's only the process you control. There are many ways to shift our emotions, like smiling, laughing, and listening to music. Find a way that works for you.

If you had some physical discomfort like a headache, you would take action to relieve it, such as taking Tylenol. Do you think about emotional pain or discomfort similarly? What actions could you take?

We may also have physical feelings in our body with certain emotions, such as muscle cramps. When you get angry, do your muscles get tense? What about when you are excited? Does your heart race? What about when you are afraid? Next time you feel a strong emotion, pay attention to your body. Different emotions can feel similar in our bodies. We need to explore how our emotions affect us.

Why are emotions so important? Emotional research shows that high awareness of our own and others' feelings is tied to greater empathy and better interpersonal effectiveness. In addition, you can have more personal satisfaction and better relationships with others (Eurich 2018). Your ability to express and control your emotions determines how well they can help you personally and professionally.

For example, could you create emotions that could fuel your performance in a piano recital? Imagine yourself more relaxed, confident, and in the flow. Envision effortless work where challenges and skills align perfectly, and time seems to stop.

*Spiritual* dimensions describe the intangible and immeasurable elements influencing your attitudes and behaviors. This can connect to what you do, how you do it, and ultimately who you are. It involves your purpose, mission, values, gifts, and beliefs concerning what you want and how you see yourself accomplishing your goals. This also can mean the connection to something bigger than yourself.

*Spiritual* is different from *religious*. Religion is a set of beliefs and practices that individuals follow together, not set by the individual.

The spiritual dimensions are individually set, and they have the potential to increase or decrease depending on beliefs about your spiritual aspects. These dimensions can inspire and motivate you.

Awareness of spiritual influence is a conscious choice for yourself. It is about thinking about how you would like to be remembered, not just about what you do, but who you are. Another way to think about this is your mission and purpose; it is a way to determine your contribution in life and what is important to you.

Think of a time when you were aligned with your mission and purpose. What were you doing? How did you feel? Were you looking forward to it?

I had the opportunity to create my mission and purpose by not being offered a partnership in a multispecialty practice. Initially, I was devastated, but I soon realized I could do it independently, without people dictating what I should and should not do. I had a few disagreements with my colleagues on what patients I should operate on. When I thought someone was not a good candidate for a refractive surgery case, my colleague decided to perform the surgery without notifying me. When I confronted him, he said, "You are not hungry enough!" Then I realized that a medical decision should not be based on my circumstances but on the integrity of doing the right thing at the right time. I have learned what not to do. This gave me the motivation to do the right thing whenever possible. Some things could not be undone. This value of integrity gave me the power to set up my practice.

*Social* needs and desires vary significantly among different individuals. Most of the discussions so far have been internal and based on individuals. Social has to do with an external focus related to people around you. It would be best to determine how much and what types of interaction suit you. Some introverted people may be comfortable working alone or in a small group, while some extroverted people would enjoy being a part of a larger group or team. What appeals to you? Create the social conditions that will work for you.

According to a book on happiness, the Harvard Study of Adult Development discussed that relationships are the key to living happy, satisfying, and healthy lives (Waldinger 2023). It also reveals that the strength of our connections with others can predict the health of our bodies and brains. In other words, the strength of our relationships with others determines how happy we are.

Communication is critical to a good relationship. Communication flows in two directions, but listening skills are generally more essential than the expressive part of communication. Words are only 7 percent of the components of face-to-face conversation; 38 percent is vocal tones, and 55 percent is nonverbal body language (Mehrabian 1972).

How often have you been in a conversation where you want to get your point across instead of genuinely listening? After you walk away, can you recollect anything the other person said?

I listen with my ears, eyes, and heart when I am present in the moment. My ears listen to your tone and your words. With my eyes, I watch your facial expressions and your body language. I listen to your feelings, emotions, and values with my heart. I also quiet my brain from making judgments, analyses, and criticism. Listening this way makes me feel more alive and helps me appreciate the other person.

The social dimension is a preference, and no judgment should be involved, such as right or wrong, good or bad. Suppose you are evaluating a relationship that drains your energy most of the time. Occasionally, the relationship can be changed by changing your perspective and mindset, but you can also consider leaving the relationship if it is an option.

## Values

Although values can belong to the spiritual part of yourself, they are important enough to be a separate section.

Setting up a new practice led me to think about my values. What do you value? What is important to you? What do you stand for? I recommend about three to five values that are important to you now. Write them down and look at them for inspiration. These values can also give you meaning and principles too.

Here are some examples: accomplishment, achievement, adventure, affiliation, appearance, autonomy, community, competency, compassion, cooperation, courage, creativity, determination, education, effort, empathy, equality, excellence, family, flexibility, freedom, friendship, fun, gratitude, growth, health, honesty, independence, integrity, justice, kindness, leisure, love, peace, power, prestige, purpose, recognition, reputation, security, success, travel, and wealth.

This list is not meant to be comprehensive. Use the values that feel true to you and add your own to this list.

Consider what is important to you and how often your actions reflect that. You want your thoughts and actions to be aligned. Values are important to consider since they help determine your priorities, direction, and motivation. These matter to you. Sometimes you have values, but you may not be able to act on them. How does that make you feel? How would you feel if your values were honored by creating action plans? How much more powerful would you feel?

> **You can start creating your purpose by choosing your values, determining what is essential, and committing to yourself.**

Values can change as you go through life-changing events, such as marriage, having a family, moving to a new place, starting a new job, and retirement. Whenever these events occur, review your values again to ensure your values are still relevant and working for you.

My values changed multiple times, in retrospect. I did not know how and when to reevaluate my values. I valued achievement, competency, and excellence when I was young, especially in my schooling years and as a trainee. Whether I was ready or not, when my family came, I had to value family, kindness, and love and not put so much value on achievements and competence. As I get older, I have placed more excellent value on health, self-care, and love.

You can start creating your purpose by choosing your values, determining what is essential, and committing to yourself. Emotions are closely linked to our values. Sometimes we react emotionally toward a person, event, or place when our values are in play. If your actions are in sync with your values, they can strengthen each other, but if they are in conflict, you may experience more self-doubt and anxiety.

While running my own practice, I attended meetings through the American Association of Physician Leadership, where they offered management and leadership courses. I never learned business finances, communication, negotiation, and leadership skills since these classes were not taught at the medical school. By taking these classes, I could also become a certified physician executive (CPE). The program required recommendation letters and was selective.

I was invited to participate in the capstone process, the last part of becoming a CPE. At that time, I had a chance to consider what I valued, which turned out to be integrity, trust, and respect. These values were the foundation of my philosophy at the time. The overarching goals are excellence and success for myself and others around me, which I aim to achieve throughout my career. My leadership style is to empower people, connect them in a team, and use collaboration. I grew up always being ingrained to do my best and pursue excellence. As I kept learning, I realized the importance of empowering the best people with resources and connecting them in teamwork and collaboration.

The next chapter will cover self-awareness. Knowing yourself is crucial to developing who you want to become. Where do you want your focus and attention to be? How will you spend your time?

**CHAPTER 3**

# Your Awareness

*The unexamined life is not worth living.*

—Socrates

Looking inward has a long tradition in Western philosophy, starting with Socrates. Your internal self-awareness is the absolute core. In ancient Greece, the philosopher Socrates declared that the unexamined life is not worth living. What exactly does that mean? Why does self-knowledge or self-awareness matter? How would you consider Socrates' aphorism "know thyself"? It is open to many different interpretations. According to Socrates, true wisdom is knowing what you do and do not know. As a result, knowing yourself includes the limits of your own wisdom and understanding. One of these facets is acknowledging your limitations and owning them.

Socrates established an ethical system based on human reason. He believed that human choices are motivated by the desire for happiness. Knowledge allows a person to reason and make choices that will bring happiness. Happiness does not come from external rewards or accolades. It is from the personal, internal success that people bestow upon themselves.

However, many of our thoughts and actions are on autopilot, which means that our habits, impulses, and reactions become automatic, so we do not stop to think about them. Do you know that an average adult makes more than 35,000 decisions per day (Zak 2020)? On a given day, people deal with simple and extraordinarily stressful and impactful decisions.

The quality of these decisions should be your focus, not the quantity. Of course, there are some simple decisions you automatically answer. However, there are some difficult decisions you may need a considerable amount of energy and time to make.

Listening to yourself is the first step to being self-aware. At first glance, there may not be much difference between reflection and introspection. Reflection means holding up a mirror that reflects what you are doing. For example, what would you notice if someone just held up a mirror in front of you that replayed the last hour of your time? It would show what you just did. You may notice that your actions were not what you wanted. Looking at yourself may show your hesitation or your feelings not being aligned. Alternatively, you may be happy with yourself. That was precisely what you wanted. Imagine if everything you have done today is exactly what you had in mind, how powerful and purposeful today could be!

Introspection is a deeper and more personal form of reflection, where you analyze and understand your situation, what emotions you felt, and why you took your actions. It is looking at your personal knowledge, including recognizing and understanding your thinking and feeling. It leads to higher levels of self-awareness and is more meaningful.

According to Eurich, there are correct and incorrect ways of performing introspection. For example, it isn't helpful to ask yourself *why me?* You may feel depressed or sad that you have been recently diagnosed with breast cancer or experienced a death in the family. *Why*s allow you to create alternative stories that may not lead you to the truth, and lead to feelings of pity for yourself. One of the dangers of introspection is that it can lead to rumination or rehashing memories over and over (Eurich 2017).

> **Be open and curious about who you are and who you want to be. Let go of any judgment about yourself.**

Instead of *whys*, ask *what about me?* It has more potential for positivity as you consider your attitudes, beliefs, and mindset. What's most important to me now? Change *why* to *what* and *how*. What did I learn that I did not know before? How did I act during the event? How can I use this experience to further my learning and growth? It is up to us to learn and grow from our mistakes, tragedies, and successes.

There are two different kinds of self-awareness: internal and external self-awareness. Internal self-awareness is how you view yourself, and external self-awareness is how others see you. Be open and curious about who you are and who you want to be. Let go of any judgment about yourself. Make a note to yourself of what triggers positive feelings. Write them down. Ask others how they see you. Ask them in what situations you shine. Be brave enough to get feedback about various situations. Many different assessments are available to understand oneself and how others see you. Some assessments on how others see you are called 360-degree assessments. 360-degree assessments are performance management tools intended for someone to get multi-source feedback on their performance and improvement areas.

## Internal Self-Awareness

Internal self-awareness occurs when you examine all parts of yourself, such as your thoughts, feelings, emotions, beliefs, values, and actions. This includes both self-reflection and introspection. Some of these areas may not be conscious or intentional unless you take the time to ask yourself. You may have acted out of habits rather than conscious thoughts. You can respond to events effectively if you are more aware of what is happening now. This allows you to create a different outcome by using actions based on adjusting your thoughts and emotions.

If you want to understand yourself, including your emotions, practice seeing your emotions' impact as it occurs. This allows you to expand on predispositions, thoughts, emotions, and actions. Your mental and emotional state may have caused specific actions.

Introspection on our successes and failures can be revealing. What strengths, weaknesses, and patterns are revealed, and how would you do something differently if you had another chance? When you undergo self-reflection and introspection to get insights, you become more aware of yourself by asking yourself whether the response made sense. Would you change the response if you had another occasion for a similar situation? Think of this as metacognition, thinking about the thinking itself. What do I feel, and what thoughts are coming up now?

Self-awareness is a lifelong journey. Practicing, observing, thinking, and having challenging conversations can take many months. Step outside yourself. How would you feel to meet yourself? How would you describe yourself as an observer? Awareness can bring up our past conditioning. If you recognize that the current conditions are like the past and want a different outcome, you must make other choices to create a different result.

At times, things happen that are beyond our control. It may not be just happening to you. For example, you or someone you know gets hurt in a car accident. Bad things can happen to anyone, and not taking things personally can be difficult. However, not taking things personally can allow you to move forward and see things differently. Perhaps you realize that things could have been much worse as you realize the damage to the car. Shift from thinking that things are happening to you to believing that things are happening without judgment. How could that shift your mindset when you no longer waste energy on unnecessary judgments?

**External Self-Awareness**

External self-awareness means how others see you. Asking others like your family, peers, friends, and mentors how you appear and being open to candid, critical, and objective perspectives will provide new insights. Be sure to ask your loving critics, those with your best interest in mind who will tell you the truth. Ask for regular feedback from work as well. Asking for three to five adjectives to describe you can be easier for others to do. Write down some of the feedback from others and compile it. Look for any similarities.

Sometimes internal and external awareness can appear as opposite or competing viewpoints. Do your best to align the similar views. By becoming more aware of yourself, you can have more influence on others and more confidence to succeed in your performance and relationships.

If you have internal self-awareness but have no external self-awareness, you may have large blind spots. Your blind spots create the difference between your actual and intended behavior. If others misunderstand your actions, then that could be frustrating to you.

How you assess yourself can differ from others who assess you. By human nature, you may be unable to eliminate your blind spots. However, changing your routine sometimes helps you to discover new insights. For example, when you try to use the other hand to brush your teeth, you realize that even a simple task is no longer routine. Do not be afraid to ask for help; pay attention to how others approach similar situations, especially when challenges arise. By being more aware of how others see you, you can overcome some limits to be more successful in your performance and relationships.

You may get frustrated with your performance and relationships if you do not have much internal and external self-awareness. Unfortunately, more experiences do not translate to more awareness. They may confirm what you think you already know. Similarly, the more power you hold does not translate to more awareness.

One day, when I walked into my clinic, a patient remarked, "It is so good to see the spring in your walk, doctor." This remark got me thinking about what percentage of the time my walk has that energy and how I want to appear for my patients. I thanked the patient for the observation, which motivated me to appear more confident and deliberate in all my activities.

Generally, it is easier to see other people's blind spots than your own. It takes some humility and willingness to be open-minded. The mind is not very good at learning new things. It automatically finds things to confirm what it already knows. Accept yourselves as a whole unit, meaning both the good and the bad of your personality, and stop judging your negative traits and characteristics. However, you may also choose to correct or modify your behaviors.

External awareness can be challenging to understand and swallow. When I invited my staff to be honest and give me feedback on both positive and negative actions I took in my business and practice, I realized my blind spots and weaknesses. I also asked them to use neutral language to eliminate any judgments, such as right, wrong, good, or bad. Getting positive feedback is easy, but hearing potentially negative insights can be difficult, but I was appreciative and able to learn and grow.

As a physician, I have made judgments about someone quite quickly without thinking. Most of the time, I was great at it since that is how I got trained in my medical career. When we have patients to care for at night on call or in a busy clinic, doctors are forced to make a judgment call. However, my staff has pointed out that my initial impressions are sometimes incorrect. After the discussion, I was more open to rethinking my impressions and allowed more of my staff's input. It helped me become a better physician.

> **Self-awareness aligns you with your values, motivations, and goals.**

### Why Is Awareness So Important?

Self-awareness involves honesty with yourself and not living with avoiding negative feelings, such as sadness, guilt, and pain. Opening yourself to all human experiences, not only positive feelings like joy and love, will allow you to live a fuller life of meaning and purpose. You can shift your priorities and direction to what is essential to you. Self-awareness aligns you with your values, motivations, and goals.

Living with awareness is investing your time and energy in yourself by balancing the internal understanding of yourself with how you appear in the external view of yourself. People who are more self-aware are happier, make smarter decisions, and have better personal and professional relationships. In addition, they are more creative and confident and are better communicators (Eurich 2017). On the flip side, a lack of self-awareness can be risky at best, and disastrous at worst. In business, our success depends on understanding who we are and how we come across to others.

Remember, focusing more on the present state can create happiness, whereas considering past or future struggles, arguments, and stress can make you feel powerless. Only being fully present at the moment will allow you to make choices.

You can become more confident and creative when you see yourself fully. You make sounder decisions, build stronger relationships, and communicate more effectively. Self-congruence is when what you say, think, and feel are consistent within yourself. When you have both internal and external self-awareness, you can fully realize the benefits of self-awareness. This can make you more confident in connecting with others. Self-awareness brings higher job and relationship satisfaction, personal and social control, and happiness. It is negatively related to anxiety, stress, and depression (Eurich 2018).

When I owned my practice, I was the owner, administrator, manager, and physician. I wanted to create my destiny instead of having a large academic center or a multiple-specialty clinic setting rules for me. Initially, I needed to learn and pay attention to many things. As an entrepreneur and owner of my practice, I realized that compensation was necessary, but there were other ways to motivate my employees. Celebrating birthdays, recognizing teamwork, and setting a positive work culture have a huge impact with minimal financial costs. Appreciation and social recognition are meaningful and rewarding for the employees. My growth in internal and external self-awareness helped me realize this and implement what I was learning.

# CHAPTER 4

# Your Authenticity

*The most common form of despair is not being who you are.*
—Søren Kierkegaard

According to existentialism, we exist first and then spend the rest of our lives creating who we are. We do not discover ourselves as we make choices for ourselves. We intentionally choose who we become. According to Sartre, "We are our choices." Authenticity involves the awareness that you are always free to transform your life through your decisions. Sartre explains further that, as humans, we have freedom of choice and are responsible for our actions and decisions.

Most existentialists believe intensity and commitment are central to being an authentic self. Authenticity requires the lucid awareness of one's responsibility for one's choices in shaping one's life. Although there are some differences in terminology depending on the individual existentialists, their commitments, values,

HAPPY SUCCESSFUL YOU

*I want to be the best version of myself!*

or passion are critical for them, from infinite passion (Søren Kierkegaard), resoluteness (Martin Heidegger), and joy of existence (Simone de Beauvoir). All of this gives life meaning. This intensity is only possible when you have a specific life-defining commitment that gives focus and a sense of direction.

Therefore, authenticity is how we view ourselves as the responsible agent for our lives, commitments, and values, individually and in our relations with others. Philosophy can help us solve today's problems; existential philosophy can be a stimulus to critical thinking and understanding of our and society's values, injustices, and oppression (Bamford 2019).

Here is my definition of authenticity, which will guide the rest of the discussion in this chapter: Being authentic is being the best version of yourself. Since no one in the world has your gifts, experiences, and style, the most potent inspiration must come from within. Authenticity is being true to you and the whole of you, regardless of the pressure that you may be under.

> **Since no one in the world has your gifts, experiences, and style, the most potent inspiration must come from within.**

## Developing Your Authenticity

By developing your natural style, beliefs, and social preferences to the best of your ability, you are searching for a satisfying and fulfilling life. Be honest with yourself and others and take responsibility for your decisions. It is up to you to develop these qualities. Who else can you be other than yourself? Learn what it means to be you and how to express your true self. Live and lead the way that matches your natural style, beliefs, and social preferences. Being yourself should feel effortless since you are the only person who can be you. Learn your strengths, gifts, and qualities so that expressing them will be natural and you can be your best.

Each of you has your path to walk. No one else can walk your path since everyone has unique backgrounds, experiences, and skills. Of course, you won't be sure where it will lead you, but by living your life more intentionally and intensely, you can choose and make your life the way you want it. Each person's best self will look quite different from other people. This is because each person has different talents, assets, and qualities. When someone finds meaning in life, that same meaning may not work for others.

Authenticity is less about the destination and more about the journey or the process. Accepting who you are and communicating who you are effectively adds value to life. It will add to your fulfillment, happiness, and satisfaction.

Remember to make your own choices and become the person you want to be as you get more experience. You can also make choices to change at any time. It is empowering! Consider your life as a journey for your self-development. It will be a rewarding experience as you learn to grow and overcome your challenges and barriers. You are not stagnant if you allow yourself to keep growing. Express your strengths and values, and allow yourself to make choices based on them. Your authenticity will become evident as you grow through life transitions.

A client of mine wanted to be more authentic and desired strategies for the next stage of his life. This person needed more confidence and wanted to learn to make meaningful connections with the appropriate leaders. He started with an awareness of himself, his surroundings, and how others saw him. As a result, he made conscious choices and was more comfortable in the present moment as things unfolded. By focusing his energy and attention on what mattered to him and what he could control, he learned not to squander precious resources.

This client had to learn to accept his past and the emotions as they showed up. With practice, he learned to use more nonjudgmental language and not take things so personally. He discovered why feelings were there and learned to accept them, which helped him become the person he wanted to be. He became much calmer, more confident, and fearless by not worrying about the future. Once he understood how to connect with someone by looking at the other person's perspective and priorities, he communicated more effectively and became more authentic.

**Visioning Exercise**

Let's begin figuring out who you are and what you want by combining some of our earlier discussions. What does your dream life look like? In your dream, what are you doing?

- What are your achievements?
- Review your strengths; what comes naturally?
- Who do you work and spend time with?
- What are the most important places in your life?
- What gives you meaning? What makes life worth living?
- Describe how you would feel and act once you achieved your dream life.
- What would be different today if you believed that you could do it?
- What would be the first few steps in that direction?

It may take time to be able to give compelling answers to each of these questions. That's okay. Remember, authenticity is a journey. Write some of the answers that resonate with you on a vision board.

A vision board has words or images of your goals and wishes to serve as motivation or inspiration. Keep this handy to review whenever you feel lost or unsure about achieving your goals.

## Imposter Syndrome

Imposter syndrome is the persistent inability to believe that one's success is deserved or has been legitimately achieved because of one's efforts or skills. If you have impostor syndrome, you will have self-doubt and feelings of personal incompetence or inadequacy, despite your education, experience, and accomplishments. You will feel like a fraud because you have not mastered what you believe you should have. When impostor syndrome was first conceptualized, it was viewed as a phenomenon common among high-achieving women. Two clinical psychologists, Pauline Rose Clance and Suzanne Imes, first identified and named the phenomenon in 1978 (Tulshyan 2021; Saymeh 2023).

Both genders are affected with imposter syndrome, which more commonly occurs in new environments, academic settings, the workplace, social interactions, and relationships (Saymeh 2023). In relationships, people with this syndrome feel they do not live up to the expectations of their friends or loved ones. As a result, they feel or experience unworthiness or feel not deserving of the benefits of the relationship.

Surveys show varying amounts of the US population suffer from imposter syndrome, with young people from eighteen to twenty-four years old suffering more of these feelings. It is common at a new job since people are unsure of their expectations of themselves and the expectations of others. In a 2020 review, 9 to 82 percent of people experience imposter syndrome, depending on who participated in these studies (Bravata 2020). The study acknowledges that the prevalence rate is variable depending on the recruitment process (e.g., population-based evaluations, studies of students, screening tools used, and the cutoff used to assess symptoms). It also notes that reporting of imposter syndrome may be subject to publication bias.

Many people experience symptoms for a limited time, such as in the first few weeks of a new job. However, in others, the experience can last for most of life. Due to this self-doubt and fear, they hold themselves back and avoid seeking higher achievements. Because of this, some have continuous cycles that reinforce imposter syndrome.

Living an inauthentic life by giving into impostor syndrome is detrimental to individuals in a practical way. Since people may not appreciate their roles, they are always in fear of themselves being discovered. In addition, they cannot relax due to self-doubt.

For example, when a medical student becomes a resident, she may have difficulty realizing that she has mastered everything she needs to move on. No one expects her to regurgitate everything she learned, only that she has learned enough knowledge and skills to move on to the next stage. You never learn everything. You are constantly learning. That's a reality we each need to accept.

Now as an intern or resident, she is officially a physician. She is now called a doctor, and other people's expectations can be too great to accept. As a trainee, she has more senior physicians to call on. Now she must trust herself and initiate assistance to her patients. She will have opportunities to learn and grow the more she tries to do.

When I set up my practice and became a CEO, I doubted my business skills since running a business was not taught in medical school. I had relatively little or no issues about being an ophthalmologist, but I did not know about writing business plans, getting loans, or reading financial spreadsheets. I was able to ask for help and learn. I did not feel like an imposter since I did not claim to be an expert. However, I was the CEO and was expected to know more than I did. Many people frequently land a job where they may have the education, knowledge, skills, and experience needed, but most of us also need to learn more when we start a new position.

According to existentialism, your authentic life requires three conditions. First, you have the freedom to make choices and to develop your unique strengths; second, your authentic life requires commitments and values that fit who you are; and third, you take full responsibility for your thoughts and actions. If you have the above conditions, then you are being authentic.

However, if you are not free to make choices in your life, or you cannot make your commitments and values, or take responsibility for your own life, then you are not being authentic. Some people live by false values they do not honestly believe.

Considering this accessible path to authenticity, I urge you not to live in another's shadow, suffer from imposter syndrome, or live inauthentically.

How do you stop thinking like an impostor? Mentally rehearsing, thinking of it as a practice run, will help you build confidence. Changing your thought process leads to changes in behavior. In some cases, people need to build resilience. Some of these will be discussed later in the book.

If you genuinely believe in the authentic you, you will not succumb to impostor syndrome. Of course, you may have some challenging days. We all do. When that happens, think about when you feel you are at your best. This helps always doing your best to become ingrained. By the definition of imposter syndrome, you cannot be an imposter when you are feeling great and doing your best.

As a surgeon, I perform the surgery in my mind on my way to the surgical center, especially for complex or unusual cases. It helps me gain confidence before I perform surgery. In addition, introspection on my finished cases has helped me review what I could have done better to be a better surgeon for future cases. The more I've had the opportunity to do these exercises, the more natural they've become. My self-awareness going to and from the surgical center has become a part of my surgical routines.

Despite all the planning, of course, I am not perfect. Occasionally, some surgeries do not go as intended. However, due to the awareness of when things may go awry, I can be more alert, and I know better how to recover when things happen. There can never be too much planning.

## Authentic, Conscious Decisions

Authentic decisions align with your values and principles and the belief that you are doing your best. These decisions inspire high integrity, trustworthiness, and confidence since you believe that these decisions are right, without any selfish or ulterior motives.

Being fully present at the moment is also influential in making decisions. Think of a recent decision. Consider what it feels like to have a choice in the decision-making process. Then consider if you did not have a choice in the matter. How would that make you feel? Remember that you always have a choice in how you react to any person, place, or thing. Pause to come up with an authentic response.

With authentic decisions, you must ask what responsibilities or consequences you create for yourself. How do you know they are right? Now you need to consider principles. What principles do you live by? For example, if you believe in acting in people's best interests, who decides what those interests are? Is it the individuals who are involved or the leader of the group?

> **Authentic decisions align with your values and principles and the belief that you are doing your best.**

How should you test your decisions? Is this decision consistent with my values and principles? If not, ensure your values have not changed. What are your current nonnegotiable values or principles?

Consider some of these ethical questions:
- Will my decisions or actions improve the world?
- If someone brought up what I did or if I knew my actions would end up on the front page of tomorrow's newspaper, would I do the same thing (Middleton 2016)?

- What would happen if everyone made the same decision I am making? What consequences would there be, if any?
- What are the best- and worst-case scenarios?

Sometimes we must ask, am I the best person to make this decision? Is this the best time to make this decision? If the answer is no, delegate to someone who can and time it accordingly. To make effective decisions, you need to understand their consequences. You can get deeper into the answers by asking the same questions repeatedly and thinking about what happens afterward.

For example, when the federal government mandated electronic health records (EHR), it incentivized providers to join early. I decided to have my practice participate. I had to buy hardware and software for every room and train all our staff. We had to cut our patient load by less than 50 percent and struggled badly for the first few days. Even after a month of using the EHR, we could not see the level of patients we used to see before having this computer system because we spent twenty to thirty minutes sharing learning from the previous day with all our staff, which was quite informative and encouraging.

After a year, our staff and I improved at using the EHR and celebrated our success when we received our first-year incentive. It was not only the incentive we were hoping for. We also realized we enjoyed having a computer system in every room because we felt that we could do much more in the room than ever, not only the exam. Access to management software, such as appointments, scheduling, patient billings, and financial information was a big plus. Since the rules for reporting have changed every few years, not being tied to the outcome and having our own goals allowed us to succeed.

When discussing your success, you need to know what success will look like. Keep in mind that each of us is different. What does success look like during the process and after? What feelings of satisfaction and fulfillment are you looking for?

Success will not look perfect or permanent. It is the process of moving in the direction you want to go. Learn to celebrate the process not the outcome. You will be happier with the process.

**CHAPTER 5**

# Making Meaningful Connections

*Only through our connectedness to others can we really know and enhance the self. And only through working on the self can we begin to enhance our connectedness to others.*

—Harriet Lerner

We are socially, emotionally, and biologically wired for connection. Some may be looking for spiritual connection as well. Some may even have a fear of disconnection. Sometimes we want connection so much that we try to be someone else because we feel that image may be more accepted. Social media depicts what and who is more popular, strengthening the pull to be inauthentic.

HAPPY SUCCESSFUL YOU

*I love my friends!*

MAKING MEANINGFUL CONNECTIONS

When situations highlight your uniqueness or differences, how do you display them as strengths? Listen to your heart. When you listen to your brain, do you recognize that you are afraid of rejection? Our hearts can extend compassion and empathy to deepen our connections.

> **Our hearts can extend compassion and empathy to deepen our connections.**

As an Asian immigrant family, specifically a Korean American family, my parents did not believe everything was possible for me, especially in the US. They felt out of place as foreigners and felt restrictions around them. They experienced financial concerns, language constraints, and cultural limitations around our family. It was difficult for me, as I did not share those feelings. I felt liberated and fought against many restrictions. My parents preferred that I speak Korean at home because they feared I would lose the language. Code-switching is when someone switches between languages. I felt that when I came home, not only did the language switch, but I felt I was almost a different person.

Now I accept my parents because they truly worked hard to assimilate in the US with their limited resources. I have become much more understanding and appreciative of everything they have done for our family. This has allowed me to not judge myself, my parents, or our situation. I accept it as is, not as good or bad, right or wrong.

How would it feel to relinquish your expectations and truly embrace who you are now? What are you left with if you embrace yourself as having done your best under all the circumstances?

Explore your roles and relationships in the next section to learn how to connect. How can you connect more deeply with kind, compassionate, and empathetic approaches with others?

## Roles and Relationships

We all play different roles in home and work life. What roles do you play in your life? Recognizing all of your roles opens up the possibility for more connections in life because we can relate to others in similar roles. For example, as a parent, I had opportunities to meet other parents.

I chose to be a physician, meaning I had to attend medical school after college. After medical school, physicians have internship and residency, adding three to seven more years, depending on the specialty. I chose ophthalmology, which had one year of internship and three years of residency. During that time, I had little control over my schedule, and I worked long hours.

As an ophthalmologist, I became more precise in work, in addition to being a detail-oriented person. Most of our surgeries are under the microscope, so precision became one of my words of choice. In refractive surgery, a ten-to-twelve-micron difference means a whole diopter of vision change. (A human hair is about seventy microns thick; one diopter of vision loss is losing the ability to focus about one meter away.) One of my favorite elements of ophthalmology is performing surgeries to enter the intricate parts of the eye and choosing to make changes in the eyes to improve vision.

I became a mother during my internship, which was a massive role. Playing with or caring for my infant at home was different from work. Precision did not work well for my infant at home. I chose flexibility as my word at home. I often had to say aloud, "I am home now," as if I would magically change by saying that, but the verbal reminders helped me focus on who I needed to be. Of course, I am the same person, but I learned to be more agile, adaptable, and patient. I learned that patience really is a virtue.

Having that experience of being a mom helped me be a better person at work too. I became more understanding, tolerant, and capable than I ever dreamed. If I had remembered authenticity, as defined here, I could have been more successful at making conscious choices. However, I did not know then what I know now. I struggled to survive, not thinking in terms of choices. I felt I had no choice, but now I believe that was my choice.

I realized I had several roles as a physician, mother, and wife, which are all demanding, so intensity and commitment became essential to display. I realized that I could not be in two places at once. I had to choose what was important at the moment and what I needed to do over everything else.

As a mom, I had the opportunity to connect with other moms through sports, like swimming, track, and cross country, since my children participated and I volunteered to help. In addition, all of my children learned to play instruments, joined the orchestra, and did other extracurricular activities, so I have helped host meets, competitions, and other events with other parents.

I thought my first job as an ophthalmologist in a major academic center was what I wanted to do. After I started, I learned that the workplace needed to know six weeks before canceling a clinic. As a mom of young kids, planning anything six weeks in advance was difficult. The kids' schools did not inform me in advance about the class performances the kids participated in, which meant that I missed most of those events. My academic work schedule did not work well when my children got sick.

I left that job to create a better life for the children and me. I chose to start a private practice to set my hours and make the money I wanted. Luckily, money followed when I saw patients, and I did not have to chase money.

Work-life balance became hugely influential as my family grew to three children. My values changed to reflect what was necessary, and I had to change my values to one set that would work for both work and life. My new set of values was integrity, agility, and excellence. Doing the right things, demanding excellence to the best of my ability, and having agility between work and life was what worked for me.

Improving relationships in all these roles requires commitment to that relationship and acceptance of who the other person is. Making a conscious effort to connect is essential. Finally, contributing to the relationship is critical. It helps to be willing to give something to build the relationship, from time, effort, and other contributions. Commit, connect, and contribute to improving any relationship.

Remember that we have our entire lives to become the person we want to be. We can make different choices at any time to create a different outcome. Significant life changes and transitions, such as a new baby or job, are the best opportunities to reassess and reset priorities. Ask yourself what your new values and priorities are to guide you toward a more fulfilling life.

## Work-Life Integration

What is work-life balance? There is no balance between work and life. If I do eight hours of work, do I do eight hours at home? Balance almost sounds confrontational and competing. With balance, whenever there is a tilt toward one side, you feel obligated to make it up. We need to do both work and life, which should be integrated. Therefore, I use the term work-life integration. Sometimes your actions in one role can affect the other. For example, I became an eye doctor for many other parents and families. When they visit, I may discuss our kids and issues at school.

If you are a woman at home, you may act as a wife, mother, daughter, and sister. It is not a simple task to keep every role separate. You may also wear several hats at work in this complicated world, such as a physician, clinic director, and committee chair.

One may argue that integration may sound almost like merging the two where there should be a boundary. I agree that there should be boundaries between work and home. However, we have the same values, priorities, and motivations wherever we go. One domain can affect others, and creatively integrating your priorities makes sense. Remember that tilting to one side is normal and natural. You can only do one thing at a time and are only one person.

At home, I realized I do not need the perfection needed in my work. It is best if I go with the flow. It is not easy to plan anything when you have three young kids. We tried football games on Saturday afternoons and free orchestral concerts as a family, but whenever the kids were ready to go, it was the right time to go.

I was grateful that we lived in a college town that allowed us to try many new activities.

Set boundaries from work and turn off technology to be fully present at home. It is amazing how a young child knows when you are working and not fully present with them. I learned to be more efficient at work, wrap up tasks more thoroughly, and anticipate issues that could arise from work. I got better at my work over time. I trained my staff to do the same and helped them prioritize their work.

Work-life integration is like the oxygen masks on a plane: secure your mask first, then assist another person. If you do not care for yourself, caring for your loved ones will be impossible when life becomes more difficult. Be aware and care for yourself, however it may look for you.

Set time for self-care. Self-care can look different for different individuals, such as mindfulness, meditation, yoga, exercise, spa, bath, sleep, *niksen* (*do nothing* in Dutch), and *fika* (*take a break* in Swedish). Figure out what works best to relax and recharge you. Remember to take care of yourself first so that you can help others.

We are constantly reminded that exercise is an essential component of a healthy lifestyle, next to a healthy diet. It is a good way of managing stress and caring for yourself. In addition, exercise minimizes the negative effects of stress, fights disease, and improves concentration, mental fitness, and cognitive function (Cairns 2021).

You may feel guilty about taking time away from others, like your children, for self-care. However, the quality of time you spend with your children matters more than the quantity of time. If you are unhappy, how would that show up when you are with your children? What about when you look forward to being with your children as you get off work an hour early? Imagine the scenarios for both situations. How do you show up for your family?

**Kindness**
When you do good things for others, you strengthen your social interactions, making you feel good. Humans like doing nice things because we are social creatures. Consider incorporating acts of kindness into your daily life. There are plenty of opportunities. Holding a door open for someone with a stroller, in a wheelchair, or with bags is a friendly, kind gesture.

When I arrived in the US with my family at age ten, I was shocked that everything seemed so different with a new language and culture. However, I realized the universal language of kindness. I had strangers who would smile and offer their assistance, teachers who would volunteer to spend extra time to teach me English, or friends who opened their hearts and minds to accept me as I am. I felt kindness, and I understood without saying anything. Of course, not everyone was kind, but I learned being kind to each other is the key to our world.

Therefore, when I had my children and my family, I taught them the most important rule: Be kind. I used to tell them that kindness makes the world go around. Being kind to each other, kind to others, and kind to yourself is an essential skill. Kindness is a universal language, like smiling, as you can hear smiling in someone's voice.

You can give affirmations or compliments. Do you notice something that someone did well? Compliment them and let them know you noticed. Affirm someone by telling them you appreciate their honesty or ability to work with others. Sincere compliments and affirmations can go a long way.

Make a habit of sharing things when you can. There are many things you can share. For example, you can share an article that will help or entertain a friend. Whatever it is, if you know the other person will appreciate it, then share it. It can be a joke, video, food, or tickets.

Do something nice for someone. For example, does a neighbor need a babysitter? Do they have a problem they cannot fix? Volunteer to help. If you see a coworker who needs help, help them. Volunteer for a cause you are passionate about. Volunteering your time shows that you care or understand. Be a friend to someone, even for a day. Sometimes all you need is a friend. Get a gift for someone. If you are shopping, and you see something that someone you know might like, consider getting it for them.

Find something you think will make a difference in someone's day. When they look back at their day, they will recognize it as kind, memorable, special, and joyous. When you brighten someone's day by being kind, you become happier by putting someone else's happiness before your own (Otake 2006). This is because we are connected as humans first, and sharing or showing kindness makes you happier.

Kindness is more than behavior. It is being generous, considerate, and helpful without expecting anything in return. Kindness has been shown to increase self-esteem, empathy, and compassion and improve mood. In addition, kindness can improve your brain physiologically (Siegle 2020).

## Self-Compassion and Compassion

Feeling connected to yourself and more accepting of every part of you builds a sense of connection. Connecting with others requires you to consider yourself compassionately so that you do not blame and criticize. Being kind to everyone, including yourself, is essential.

Let us first talk about you. You might believe that being critical will help you perform better. You will not slack off or rest on your laurels if you are demanding on yourself. However, research shows that if you are harder on yourself, you are more likely to struggle to be effective or stay motivated, leading to lower performance overall (Christian 2019).

Having self-compassion will pay off in the long run. Show yourself the kindness you would show to a loved one. Whenever you make a mistake or fall below your expectations, resist your urge to criticize yourself. Instead of thinking, "That was sloppy. You cannot do anything right," say something like, "It is okay. There is always next time," or, "It is all right. I just learned something new." This attitude creates trust and love for yourself, enabling you to overcome your fear of failure. As a result, you will see yourself trying more things.

> **Show yourself the kindness you would show to a loved one.**

You are often your worst critic. It is usually after an event didn't go as planned that we become the most critical of ourselves. Instead, if you can focus on the task by being present and doing your best each time, you will be able to accept the process and the outcome. If you truly give your best, there cannot be any more to give to the task.

Compassion for someone else is a feeling of sympathy and sorrow for someone stricken by misfortunes and suffering, accompanied by a desire to help them. By using the awareness of others, you can assist others. Taking care of ourselves and each other can occur through compassion. Successful relationships generally have mutual respect and enjoyment, fondness, and support for one another. Compassion promotes meaning and deeper connections to improve well-being for both people.

**Empathy**

Empathy is the ability to understand and share feelings and emotions with others. How do we relate to each other through this connection? This quality serves well for a physician. When I smile first, most of my patients return the smile. I make the effort to remember my patients' names, be open and curious about their conditions, and give full attention to assist them in many ways. I have tried to understand the patient's perspective, and they share their emotional experience. This helps me connect with them more deeply and, more importantly, creates opportunities for me to help them.

We are never in isolation. Human connection is a bond that occurs when we feel seen and valued. People exchange positive energy with one another and feel trust and even a sense of belonging. We are a social species wired to connect. It is part of our well-being as humans (Wooll 2021). For example, if you are a fan of a sports team and your team is playing, you share feelings and emotions, like excitement, joy, and pain. You may not always agree with other fans, but having the respect and humility to accept others as they are is essential.

When I examine patients, I discuss their conditions and diagnoses to give options on the treatment plans. Demonstrating that I understand their issues is a form of empathy. I discuss it to ensure the patient and family understand and agree. I have encountered cases where the patient or family may not agree with the plans. If that is the case, it does not matter how great the plan is. I connect with them to win their trust and respect by showing compassion and empathy.

In addition, through empathy, I connect with the feelings and emotions of my patients. If the patient is frustrated, in pain, or excited, I validate the feelings, showing that I understand and care. Sometimes just connecting with understanding and care may not be enough. Especially with my chronic patients, I needed to understand what motivates my patients. Empathy has allowed me to connect with some patients further regarding motivation. For my glaucoma patients, I have to rely on them to use eye medications, which is essential. I usually see them often enough that I know how to approach them on a deeper level to keep them motivated to use their medication.

Experiencing increased connectedness can lead to life satisfaction, resilience, and better mental health. A robust support system, whether a family or friends, can decrease health risks and improve physical well-being. It also strengthens the immune system and increases your chance of a longer life.

As words of caution, however, having too much empathy with negative emotions can lead to fatigue and exhaustion. This can happen in health care, and some frontline workers feel burnout when they spend too much time in this space. Unfortunately, there is grief, sadness, and loss, but it can also cause depression as well. You will not be able to sustain yourself for too long in these negative emotions. Remember to make some boundaries for yourself for your protection.

For example, during the height of COVID, hospitals were so overcrowded with COVID patients that the hospitals were not accepting other types of patients, and at times, they did not have beds to admit patients. As a result, the patients were in the hallways waiting for beds. Doctors, nurses, and hospital employees worked with these patients and their families over long days and weeks. They struggled to face anger, grief, and loss with empathy without succumbing to depression and exhaustion. Although being empathetic is generally positive, you must set boundaries to protect yourself from burnout and exhaustion. Imagine if you had these similar stories day after day. You get so completely drained that you may be unable to function properly.

I have realized that you cannot stop at compassion and empathy. We need actions to follow these feelings and emotions. Actions do speak louder than words, and they take courage. It is an opportunity to advocate for people who cannot speak for themselves. This runs into fixing problems for others, but you must also consider teaching them about their sustainability. You do not live alone, and the world has gotten smaller. You live in neighborhoods and communities and rely on others to care for your children, family, friends, and others. Making active networks and connecting with others is beneficial to life.

**Forgiveness**
Forgiveness is a skill that we can use to improve our relationships and connect with others. We all make mistakes along the way. Sometimes we hurt others intentionally or unintentionally, whether they admit it or not. Apologizing and asking for forgiveness matters. The fact that you are taking responsibility can be enough.

Forgiveness may mean different things to different people. It involves a conscious, intentional decision to relinquish your resentment and anger. By forgiving someone, you let go of your grudges and bitterness. Forgiveness is not for the benefit of the person you are forgiving. Forgiveness allows you to get rid of the burden that you are carrying. It helps you to free yourself from the control of the person who harmed you. If you feel like a victim, you carry a heavy burden. You may get stuck in the past, not able to move on.

Forgiveness can lead to understanding, compassion, and empathy for the one who has hurt you. It allows you to feel peace, joy, and love again. In addition, it improves your relationships and connectivity with others when you can forgive and let go.

When considering human connection and when we want to improve our relationships, we need forgiveness, kindness, compassion, and empathy. These relational skills improve your health and sleep, including lowering blood pressure and stress.

The first section is the process of creating you, from wherever you are at this point in your life, to become a person who can recognize new opportunities for yourself. Choosing you is to invest and develop yourself to the best of your abilities or your full potential. Introducing philosophical ideas empowers you to create meaning, self-awareness, and authenticity to be the best version of yourself. Finally, realizing that you do not live as a hermit but in a community, a society, and as a global being, we all need to connect with others and empower others to live well.

The next section discusses our work life since we spend much of our time working.

# Part II

# Finding the Work You Want

When you focus on why you are doing something instead of what you are doing, you become more motivated and find your work meaningful. For example, if you're a runner, it will be easier to sustain the behavior of running if you think about why you are running, such as cardiovascular health, physical fitness, and cognitive improvement. Finding more motivation for other activities can work similarly.

This section is designed to help you figure out your reasons for working more broadly, then find the meaning of your specific work. By thinking about the reason you work, rather than just the work itself, you can find your purpose and meaning in your work.

**CHAPTER 6**

# The Purpose of Work

*Everything can be taken from a man but one thing: the last of the human freedoms—to choose one's attitude in any given set of circumstances, to choose one's way.*
—Viktor Frankl

If your reasons for working align with your purpose for your life, you will find your work-life integration much more effective. What are some of your reasons for working? What purpose does it serve in your life?

Developing your message or what is meaningful for you is essential. For example, I do not usually consider my job as a doctor to provide health care, leading to a healthier and happier society, which may be true. I work as an ophthalmologist to help people see better. I have been nearsighted since I was eight years old, and this personal reason gets me up in the morning.

According to the Bureau of Labor Statistics (2023), most full-time job holders in 2022 worked eight hours daily, with a weekly total of about forty-two. The numbers vary depending on gender, age, and other factors. If you spend about a third of your time doing work that you do not want to do, do you really want to keep doing that? You only live once.

> **Understanding how you conceptualize work and your relationship to work is essential.**

Similar themes emerge about why people choose their jobs or careers. Let us look at several popular reasons why people choose the work they do: passion, talent, identity, and money. Understanding how you conceptualize work and your relationship to work is essential. This discussion will help you discover what you want or need from work. You may value a combination of some or all of these reasons.

## Passion

Passion for work means you are excited about what you do. You find meaning and purpose in your work. You may have chosen the work you do because of all these aspects. Passion gives you thrilling glimpses into your hidden potential and helps you realize that you can achieve more. It ignites you to take new risks and push your boundaries. At times, it infuses the work with higher creativity, brilliance, and imagination. Having multiple interests can create more opportunities (Finkelstein 2021).

Since you spend about a third of your life working, you want to enjoy what you do. When your work becomes more challenging and stressful, finding that passion in your work will invigorate you.

Some people know what they are passionate about when they are young. As you progress through life, your passions may change. I know someone who loved her violin, and she played her violin well. For years, she declared that she wanted to be a violinist. However, when she was in high school, she had the opportunity to attend an intensive music camp where she played her violin in an orchestra and took chamber music and private lessons. She practiced all day and evening except for eating and sleeping. After she returned, instead of feeling sure of herself, she decided to pursue her other interests.

On the other hand, some people's interest in music had been ignited fiercely after the same camp experience. This person wanted to practice more, wanted to perform more, and felt ready for more challenges. Whenever possible, immerse yourself into the passion to see how your experience makes a difference.

The practical reason that people follow their passion is to escape the grind. They believe the adage that if you do what you love, you never have to work a single day. These people treasure the satisfaction of working on things that kindle their heart, and some are happy about taking this route. They are happy to encourage others to follow their passion because they experience high satisfaction levels and find meaning at work. Part of this belief is that you are doing something you are meant to do.

Think of a soloist in an orchestra who loves to perform and does not mind the extra time he commits to being a soloist. Unless you are a designated soloist, your compensation for it may be ignored. To avoid these problems, passion-driven workers should set boundaries and know the value of their work. In addition, passion-driven workers may be open to accepting less compensation than their work is worth since the work itself may be a privilege enough.

Are you feeling passionate about what you are doing now? How important is it to you to enjoy and love what you do for work?

## Talent

If you are a talent-driven worker, you may follow a career based on what comes naturally to you or explore careers related to your talent. The exploration process can be organic or deliberate.

Talent-driven people are lucky because their jobs fit their strengths. If you play your cards right, you can advance quickly into desirable positions in the organizations you work for. Being exceptional at something is a currency you can use to open doors to good compensation and new opportunities.

There are two types of talent-driven people. The first type enjoys doing their work because it comes naturally to them. You find your job engaging, energizing, and fun. The pursuit of mastery and excellence is a significant motivator. You may feel like you are fulfilling a calling.

An example is someone gifted at math and computers who becomes an IT professional. They would not say they are passionate about the job, but they are good at it. Because the work is so natural to them, they can appear almost effortless. In addition, they often use their strengths, so the work is engaging and fun, so they do not mind doing extra work.

The second type of talent-driven people believe you should do what you are good at, so you have time for what you love. They do not expect work to be fun, and that is fine because work is for money. Any joy they might derive from their occupation is a happy accident. A job is supposed to support you not entertain you. You can leverage your talent to create happier and more pleasant work.

## Identity

Work identity is a part of the identity of many adults. Identity impacts the way people think and act in the context or their work. If you are motivated by your sense of identity, you are trying to answer more profound questions about your role in life and society. You may see your work as an integral part of who you are. For example, many physicians consider themselves physicians both professionally and in their personal lives. They can get engrossed in their status, especially since people see them differently once they are doctors.

Identity-driven people tend to be highly ambitious and treat work as play and a privilege. You are always working even when you are not supposed to because any moment is an opportunity to enhance your sense of self. These people are often drawn to positions like judges, senators, presidents of organizations, or board members.

For example, think of the lawyer who eats, drinks, and sleeps a case. This lawyer is ready to do whatever it takes to win this case since he has chosen being an attorney as his identity. People like them who believe their work and personal life are identical can make huge sacrifices that leave little room for life outside work. Since there is hardly a distinction between work and personal life for them, they do not feel like it's a sacrifice even when their obsession with work seems to dominate. If the lawyer loses the case, they will be devastated, and worse if they lose a couple. They might even have an identity crisis around their inability to deliver.

This type of work culture can be unhealthy and dangerous. Not sleeping enough is dangerous and is common among identity-driven workers. Neglecting other responsibilities and loved ones, often the person's entire support system, are also typical unhealthy patterns.

Without their work, they are bored, miserable, and clueless about what to do or who they are. When something goes wrong at work, it feels like something is going wrong in their whole life because there is not a clear separation between the two. Their job is who they are. Think about the last time you heard someone say their job gives them purpose and meaning. It is not a bad thing in and of itself, but it can be detrimental when work is all they have with no personal life.

A journalist may keep chasing a story for months, putting their life on pause. Likewise, journalists will feel lost and purposeless if they are suddenly fired and have to start over elsewhere. This is unnecessary spiritual and psychological pain that can be avoided by centering your sense of self and identity elsewhere.

It's good to find joy and happiness in work, but that should not come at a cost to your well-being. Work will not love you back. You cannot have your personhood tied to a profession. You are a human being before you are a professional.

## Money

Many people are motivated by money. These people conceive of a career as purely transactional. Sometimes the job may align with a person's talents, passion, or identity, but it does not have to. That is okay for them; they willingly forgo those in their work.

No one can deny the power of money. Money helps protect us and gives us the freedom to live as we desire. It is power, and those motivated by money want that power. We have all met people who have pursued a career purely because of money. Judging from the many people who want to be rich, you can bet many of us are motivated by money. In addition, there are many people who live paycheck to paycheck. For them, working is crucial to make ends meet.

Overall, money rewards accomplishment, hard work, and productivity. People will work harder and produce more if substantial financial rewards are placed before them. Money motivates people, and extra money motivates people to work extra (Minhaz 2023).

Money-motivated people must watch out for the "I get paid well" trap. It is much more difficult to leave a job that pays you well than a job that pays you less. Of course, highly skilled industries require long hours, such as investments, technologies, cutting-edge industries, and start-ups. People who work in cutting-edge industries, like tech, often fall for this trap. As a human being, it is essential to recognize your values and all the parts of yourself so that you are at peace with yourself.

A positive is that money-motivated people are more cognizant of their worth and can negotiate better terms. That proactive attitude to money and salary negotiations ensures they get a fair share. The degree to which you do this depends on your assertiveness and commitment to yourself.

## Why Do You Work?

Most people aren't motivated by only one of these as a reason for work. People combine all these reasons: passion, talent, identity, and money. Consider these four areas and ask yourself how you see yourself in these categories. If you are considering switching workplaces or careers, think about how the new place or a new career will rank in areas of passion, talent, identity, and money. For example, if the other place offers more money, but you may have a longer commute or longer hours to work, imagine yourself having worked at least a year, and compare how you would be at that point. How would you feel?

Consider all the parts of yourself. Some people choose a career for reasons unrelated to

**People combine all these reasons: passion, talent, identity, and money.**

their unique personality, interest, and skills. As we've seen with all the paths, that may be at the expense of their well-being. A mismatch between a career and passion, aptitude, or identity can be a source of anguish. For instance, if you are an environmentalist and work at a company harming the planet, you may experience moral injury. The same applies to a developer who works at a company that creates software being used to harm innocent people. The money may be good, but that mismatch between your values and the work can be harmful. A comparable dynamic can play out with passion and aptitude. Your values play a role in your alignment. If you know what is essential to you, then it will help you to stand firmly for yourself.

As mentioned, most people do not follow just one of these patterns. You can combine the reasons to fit you.

If you can find a workplace that matches your values, missions, and beliefs, then it can strengthen your values, purpose, and beliefs. For example, consider someone who has a career in finance because she has always loved business and working with clients since she helped at her dad's business as a child. She discovered early that she is good at thinking about money, making investments, and working with money. Her sense of purpose and identity are wrapped up in her career because it feels natural. This is a classic example of someone loving what they do because they are good at it and find a sense of identity in it.

**CHAPTER 7**

# Creating Meaning in Work

*If one wanted to crush and destroy a man entirely, to mete out to him the most terrible punishment ... all one would have to do would be to make him do work that was completely and utterly devoid of usefulness and meaning.*
—Fyodor Dostoevsky

Meaningful work is what most of us strive for. We want to find purpose, meaning, and direction in our work. That sense of meaning makes the work you do worth doing. You may have never thought about it consciously, but you've likely thought about the value of doing your work and why you do it.

How do you add meaning to your work? This involves focusing not only on what you do, but why or how you do it. Are you able to come up with a new angle? What would that mean to you? If you have answers to these questions, then those answers can help you be more resistant to challenges at work.

HAPPY SUCCESSFUL YOU

*Why am I working? I get to create my own meaning!*

## What Makes Work Meaningful?

Meaning is important enough that nine out of ten people are willing to earn about 23 percent less money to do more meaningful work (Achor 2018). Meaningful work leads to more satisfaction and fulfillment for

> **The meaning in work is personal and individualized.**

the employees. Employees who experience strong workplace social support found more meaning.

Let us examine what makes work meaningful. No job maintains meaning in all activities, and making meaning varies according to your interpretations, situations, and events. The meaning in work is personal and individualized. In addition, you may not be consciously aware of the significance of your work at that moment, but later during your reflection and introspection you can see its value. The completed work and making connections can create a sense of meaning. Your sense of meaning is created through thoughtful introspection rather than a spontaneous emotional response. Although you may experience good feelings at the moment, deep meaning comes from reflection and introspection.

Employees do better when their everyday work is connected to a larger purpose. Business leaders recognize this and communicate the company's vision to their employees. The company can adjust its goals to make them more tangible and easier to connect to workers' everyday tasks. Finding a shared purpose between the organization and employees can help. Here are some common ways to make your work more meaningful.

### *See How It Matters to Another Person*

When your work matters to another person, such as a physician assisting patients or a teacher caring about students, you will likely find your work more meaningful. Your work matters a great deal to those individuals or society. When the work becomes challenging or upsetting, you can find it worth the struggle because of the impact on others.

Thinking about how your work impacts customers can add much value and meaning. Getting in contact with someone who has benefited from the product or service you provided can reinforce meaning.

As a physician, I see the effects of cataract surgery, which shows remarkable vision improvement. It is rewarding and almost addictive. I remember a case like yesterday. A granddaughter brought her grandpa in for an eye exam because she realized that her grandpa could not recognize that he already had multiple packages of chicken in his freezer. He insisted that they were beef because they looked brown to him. When I examined his eyes, he had very dense cataracts in both of his eyes. His vision was so poor, he could not even see the big E on the chart and could barely count the fingers that I held in front of him.

His world became much brighter and clearer after the first eye surgery. In the recovery room he was giddy as he noticed things around him, seeing them clearly for the first time in a long time. One of the first things the patient said to me was, "Hey, doc, you are quite pretty!" I responded, "Thank you. We have met before." We both laughed.

I love these moments of awe for patients. It really makes my day! I feel energized and engaged with my patients and grateful for their trust in me to deliver their eye care. I also make mental notes on their different situations. I savor these moments again when patients return for a follow-up. Usually, after six months or so, patients have adjusted to their new vision and forget how it made them feel. I remind them to savor these moments again, and we all get much happier!

## *Increase the Creativity*

When your work requires creativity, then you have some agency and autonomy in your work. Agency is the feeling of control over your actions and consequences, and autonomy means you can work in a way that suits you. In these jobs, you increase the chance of finding your job interesting, creative, and meaningful (Bailey 2016). Look for work that allows some agency and autonomy to use your creativity in your work.

You can do a few things to make your work more autonomous and creative. If you are in a job that does not give you the opportunity, you can ask for changes that will give you more decision-making power. You can ask for flexibility or to be involved in projects and aspects of your work that interest you more.

For example, if your goal is to improve patient care, your personal touch can go a long way. Think about what outcome you and the patient can create by the end of the visit. Would adding kindness as you work with others make you more satisfied, happy, or fulfilled?

### *Maximize Your Impact*

When your work impacts the issues you care about, you will likely find the work more meaningful. The solution is to increase your work's impact on ideas you care about. You may need to take the necessary steps to make a difference.

For example, a lawyer who cares about the environment can take more cases that protect the environment, help families affected by corporate pollution, or join organizations aligned with their values.

### *Build Personal Significance*

Sometimes it is what the job means to you and your situation that makes it meaningful. For instance, a cosmologist who has always wanted to understand the mysteries of the universe finds their work meaningful because they are fulfilling a deep curiosity they have always had.

Work is meaningful when it lets you practice your skills and talents fully. That is one of the reasons that when work is beyond your skills, you feel like your efforts are futile. When your work is beneath your skills, you feel alienated, bored, and tedious. Work that matches your capabilities is desirable for creating meaning.

If you feel your skills are underutilized, there are a few things you can do to remedy that. First, you can ask for more responsibility or more complex problems. Second, you can seek out opportunities in your workplace that require other skills you have. Finally, remind your superiors of your willingness to help when specific kinds of work arise and check in periodically.

## *Seek Recognition*

If praise and recognition are important to you, seek work in organizations with a culture of affirmation. Alternatively, you can push for such a culture in your workplace. From coworkers to team leaders and managers, everyone should be encouraged to make praise and recognition an integral part of company culture. Working at a place that already implements this culture can make it easier to find meaning.

Recognition of your work means a balance between effort and reward. This balance means you are more likely to be satisfied with your work. If you feel like you are putting a lot of effort into something and the rewards are meager, it feels like wasted potential and energy. When you feel your efforts are well spent and amount to something, you are more likely to find the work meaningful.

If you feel there is a mismatch between effort and reward, there are things you can do to remedy the situation and create a better balance. First, you can consider asking for more rewards you find meaningful, such as financial or personal. Financial rewards include flexibility, working fewer hours, and getting additional time off. Personal rewards can include opportunities to learn and develop more skills. Depending on what is important to you, you can take the necessary steps to get what you deserve or set up a reward system that makes your work worthwhile.

When your work is recognized, praised, or acknowledged by others, your work becomes more meaningful. Those people may be the general public, peers, professional guilds, or communities whose opinion matters to you. You are less likely to find your work meaningful when you think your efforts are thankless and undervalued. If you are recognized for your accomplishments, work can become more meaningful to you. Sharing your work with friends and family can help you get your desired validation.

## *Make Work Fun*

Turning mundane activities into a game can make difficult work easier and more meaningful. For instance, I have a friend who used to hate hiking. To get into it, he made up a game where he considered the shadows in his path lava, so he had to skip over them until he reached his destination. He only had three lives, and if he got there without losing all of them, he rewarded himself. He started enjoying hiking, even when he no longer needed the game.

When we see a new patient, it takes extra work by the whole team. The front desk person checks them in to get their ID and insurance card. The clinical staff must have an extensive history, including family and social history, and complete medication lists. We celebrate every fifty new patients. Creating a way to celebrate can make work fun and meaningful, from providing breakfast, snacks, or lunch. It is up to you.

The mental game you employ will make the things that have little significance to you more significant by making the process engaging and rewarding. Remember Mary Poppins's saying, "In every job that must be done, there is an element of fun." If you find the fun, the job can become a game.

What mental game can you develop to make your work more absorbing and rewarding? Use it if you can. Remember that fun is different for every individual, so ask others for their input if you are trying to create fun for a group.

## Find Your Own Meaning

All these things can be present in meaningful work, although you do not need all of them. The question is: What do you think about your work? What meaning do you derive from your current work? You have the power to imbue anything with meaning.

The secret to that power is freedom in two primary ways: freedom in your mind and freedom to act. Freedom of thought is about your beliefs, memories, and attitudes, and freedom of action is about the choices you can make to create meaning for yourself.

> **It is important to note that some components of meaningful work are more in your control than others.**

It is important to note that some components of meaningful work are more in your control than others. That has implications for the actions you take when trying to imbue your work with meaning. The more in your control work is, the more power you have to imbue your work with meaning. Not everything at work will always be meaningful, and not everyone seeks meaning the same way.

It is worth remembering that some strategies will be more applicable to your work situation than others. In some situations, you might need multiple strategies together. In some cases, one will be enough. It depends on you and your unique situation. Experiment to think of the best ways of applying the ideas to your situation. This is not meant as an exhaustive list since there are other ways to create meaning.

## Other Options

Sometimes the solution to your burnout is something more drastic, like quitting or retiring. For example, if toxic conditions at your workplace will not cease and show no signs of improvement, it might be better to quit.

Before quitting, you must think carefully about the consequences and whether you already have a position lined up. Leaving a job when you do not have a plan can be disastrous, so avoid impulsive quitting. Remember that building a meaningful life is a process that takes time. Your decision to leave should be thoughtful. It would be best to have another position lined up already. When you leave your old job, leave on good terms in case things do not work out at your next job or you need a reference. Find a new position that aligns more with your values and interests.

If you are considering a career change, do as much research as possible about transitioning to your new field. You need to know the timeline and when to expect results, so you can lay the groundwork for success. If that requires working part-time and taking classes, figure it out. You need to ensure that the problems you face in your profession are not the same ones you will face in your new career. Reflect honestly about the downsides of transitioning and the possibility of failure.

Retirement is a particular transition where everything can change for you. Initially, when I retired from ophthalmology, I was excited, and I slept a lot to catch up on rest. I also saw a lot of opportunities and possibilities to invest my skills. I traveled to build meaning in my life.

# Part III

# Tools and Skills for Sustainability

Once you've gotten to know yourself and found meaningful work, you have to maintain your success and happiness. It's not an investment you only make once. This section will explore simple tools to overcome specific challenges, such as limiting beliefs and languages. Some tools are meant to be used on a challenging day and reshelved for later, and some need to be habitual, so they need more reinforcement. We'll also see how thinking deeply about your authentic self may require more extensive habits and skills to sustain the behavior change.

Just having insights and knowledge will not create new actions. A limiting belief is a thought or state of mind that you think is the absolute truth and stops you from doing certain things. If beliefs limit you and prevent you from doing particular aspects of your life, then you should figure out how to overcome them. These beliefs are not always about yourself. They could be about how the world works and how you interact with people (Wooll 2022). Limiting language can limit our thinking. I will discuss it further in the next chapter.

**CHAPTER 8**

# Identifying and Overcoming Challenges

*Yesterday I was clever, so I wanted to change the world. Today I am wise, so I am changing myself.*

—Rumi

We all deal with challenges and barriers at work or home. You limit your potential and performance if they block your choices. This chapter will identify some everyday stressors in your life to overcome.

There are two basic types of stressors: external and internal (Segal 2021). External stressors come from the world around you, from your actions, the actions of others, or by chance. For instance, you may make a mistake that gets you in trouble, which is external stress created inadvertently by your actions. Your boss may delegate many tasks to you, which is external stress caused by someone else's actions. Someone you

HAPPY SUCCESSFUL YOU

*I am too overwhelmed with so much stress!*

love may die from a disease, which is an external stress caused by chance.

On the other hand, internal stressors are those within you that you can do something about. Although you may not be able to control all the external stressors, you can overcome most of your internal stressors.

**External Stressors**

Most external stressors are outside your control, such as economic and environmental stressors, like dealing with heat in Arizona in the summer or freezing cold in Maine in the winter. External stressors are more challenging to deal with since they are outside your control, and each situation looks different. For example, if you need skills and training, you should identify and choose to get more schooling and training. If you need capital and resources or other economic conditions, you must identify your needs and figure out how to meet them. These situations have elements you cannot control.

A significant life change, including relationship difficulties, often causes turmoil with internal and external stressors, which individuals have varying degrees of control over. People generally do not like changes, although they are a normal part of life. For example, marriage, divorce, pregnancy, raising children, changes in health for you or a family member, retirement, job loss, death, moving to a new place, or change in social activities or social circle can all cause stress. This means even positive things like an engagement or moving in together can cause stress.

Although many of these changes are external, we can look for internal components in all these events. For example, any events above can involve our thoughts, emotions, interpretations, assumption, and inner voices. If we can recognize the internal stressors, we can overcome them.

For example, everything in relationships that makes you feel uncomfortable or unhappy or puts you under pressure is a stressor. You need to examine why you feel those uncomfortable emotions. Although the events are evident, sometimes the stressors do not happen quickly, making the changes and challenges difficult to recognize.

## Internal Stressors

While you may have little control over external stressors, you have more control over internal stressors. Keep in mind that many situations have components of both internal and external stressors. To determine any internal components, ask yourself: Do I have control over this issue by rethinking my beliefs, perceptions, and mindsets? Are there any of my responsibilities here? Remember your choices and responsibilities and their consequences.

## IDENTIFYING AND OVERCOMING CHALLENGES

Getting a new role at work is a common stressor. For example, perhaps you got promoted with better pay. You may have wanted this for a while, and now you have it, but you wonder why everything is not yet better. Whenever there is a change, you may need to settle into it until you adapt. What matters is how you approach it. Do any of your thoughts on this promotion bother you? Ensure you know you deserve this promotion and do not get into imposter syndrome.

We often fail to recognize or celebrate small achievements, especially if they fall beneath our standards. This can lead to feelings of inadequacy or stagnation. However small your achievement is, you should stop, recognize, and celebrate it. Remember, the process, not the outcome, makes the difference.

Many internal stressors are caused by unhealthy, limiting patterns of thought and interpretations or perceptions of people and situations. You may assume that what you experienced before will happen again without thinking through what might be different in this case.

An inner, antagonizing voice, sometimes called a gremlin, can limit you. What does your inner voice tell you? Does it ever tell you how great you are or give you more options? Or does it say that you are not good enough, smart enough, or lovable enough? Does it lead you to a downward spiral of negativity? We all have our inner voices that continue our negative self-talk, but when we encounter internal stressors, we want to recognize them and develop inner voices that seek solutions. Here are a few common inner stressors.

## *Limiting Beliefs*

Limiting beliefs are generalizations, stereotypes, or ideas you learned and accepted to be true that could limit your potential. Limiting beliefs can be about yourself, the world, or others. For example, if you believe that successful people are just lucky, then you would not take any further actions but wait around for fortune or luck to find you. Some of these beliefs can limit your actions and sense of control.

> **Limiting beliefs can be about yourself, the world, or others.**

Have you been told that you are not athletic enough or cannot sing or act? Have you accepted that and not tried to do those things? How about if your goal is to enjoy sports more or to be able to carry a tune? Could you get better with practice?

Challenge yourself to rethink your belief. How true is the belief? What makes it trustworthy? What evidence do you have? If you do not believe it anymore, what will happen? What other ideas come up?

You may be surprised to find that your attitude can limit you. If you believe there is never enough or everyone is for themselves, you will constantly fight for things and protect yourself from others. It would be exhausting.

On the other hand, some beliefs are not limiting you. They may even inspire you, such as the belief that anything is possible. This belief opens you to more possibilities and opportunities and allows you to make more choices. Thus, this is not a limiting belief.

One of my limiting beliefs used to be that I was not ready and needed more experience. I used to avoid volunteering to do more than I had to during my schooling years. However, I had to assist my parents frequently in translating English because their language barrier was worse than mine. What I eventually realized was that not many people ever get experience before they do something. I just had to step up to translate things that I may not have even understood. The more I did it, the more comfortable I became, and I got better at it.

## *Limiting Language*

Like limiting beliefs, your language may limit your choices instead of expanding them. The language you use can either empower or disempower you and lead to feelings of hope or hopelessness.

Language is more than a way of communicating your ideas; it shapes your attitudes and thoughts.

Words like *should/should not* or *must/must not* can constrain or limit you, as well as phrases like *I got to, I have to,* or *I need to.* If you use *choose to* or *choose not to,* those words can expand your choices. You will notice that the words free you to be in the moment, and you get to decide what you want to do, which makes you more productive as you choose or reinforce what you want.

Here are some examples of common limiting language and better options.

Instead of *I should get to work on time,* how about *I want* or *I choose to get to work on time*? When you say *I want to* or *choose to,* you are empowering yourself and making an intentional plan. By using words like *want* or *choose,* you take ownership of your actions and create a more empowering mindset.

Whenever I hear *I can't,* it sounds like someone is simply giving up. I wonder if there was any engagement in the first place. However, when I heard *I chose not to take that trip,* it sounds like a person's choice.

## IDENTIFYING AND OVERCOMING CHALLENGES

How about when someone states that *things keep happening to me*? Does that sound like a view of a victim? Saying *things are happening for me* is a slight change in how you speak, but it is a powerful shift in your outlook and attitude.

*I have to get this report done* sounds heavier or more of an obligation than *I choose to get this report done*. When first trying this technique, you might encounter some resistance. You might think, *I have to get it done because I will be in trouble if I don't*. That thinking overlooks an important detail: You do not have to. You may choose not to do the report and end up in trouble. You choose not to be in trouble. That is why you are doing the report. You have an agency. The point of the exercise is to help you stay cognizant of the facts.

Many more words and phrases belong on the list above. The trick to recognizing when you use one is asking yourself: Does this phrasing expand or take away my choices? Sentences like *I have no choice* are extreme because they deny all your agency. Asking *what choices do I have?* allows you to look for options.

Remove *never* and *ever* from your vocabulary or use *yet* along with them to open your options. By being mindful of our language and making conscious choices about our words, we can expand our options, foster a more empowering mindset, and approach life with a greater sense of agency.

## *Interpretation*

We all add our interpretation of an event, situation, person, or experience based on our perceptions. We tend to color the story with opinion or judgment as we create our understanding and believe it to be true. We unconsciously look to support our view and keep believing that our story is true, although it is one viewpoint among many. We miss the chance to focus on other possibilities.

As you look for other interpretations, ask yourself: What is another way to look at that? What might the other person's perspective be? Who has an opposing viewpoint? What would a third party who observed the situation say about your interpretation? Being aware of yourself is a critical part of this process.

## *Assumption*

We may assume that a situation or outcome will happen again because it has happened in the past. This is a problem since it may limit us and prevent us from trying a similar thing again. These ideas are more difficult to let go of because they are based on personal experience, and more emotion and energy are involved.

What is blocking you from trying again? Does that make sense to you? What could you do differently this time? What have you learned that you could do differently to ensure success? Could you think of this as an opportunity to redo it? It's not too often we get a second chance in life. If you do, take advantage and practice everything you have learned since then.

As you continue to grow and change, you are not the same person who failed initially. You can consider your past successes and what you used in those cases. What comes naturally for you? First, consider what you used in the past, like your strengths, gifts, and resources. Then, you can use them again for the challenge in front of you.

## *Inner Voice or Gremlin*

Does your inner voice ever say how great you are? Do not listen to your inner voice when it says negative talk, such as that you are not good enough, smart enough, or not worthy of love. It might initially feel ridiculous, but dealing with all those disempowering voices is essential.

Your inner voice developed to prevent you from embarrassing yourself, making mistakes, or taking too many risks. One way of looking at our inner voices is that it protects us from disappointments and other negative events based on past experience. However, now you may want to choose to take a risk. You are no longer the person you were in the past. You can choose what you want, learn more, and deal with the consequences.

My inner voice used to tell me that I was not smart enough. I used to think that my older brother, who was three years older, was brilliant since that's what my parents and others around me said. I kept believing that I was not smart enough. It took me a while to realize that I did not need to be smarter than my brother. I only needed to be smart enough to do what I wanted—to make my own choices.

## *Difficulty Accepting Uncertainty*

An inability to accept uncertainty is an internal stressor. Some people fear the lack of control that comes from being uncertain. If you do not have any certainty, you cannot prepare for anything or know the right actions to take at any moment. When you decide to be brave and act in the face of uncertainty, you cannot be confident that you are making the best decision. At the center of uncertainty is a fear of choosing wrongly and making things worse. It is a human condition that we have difficulty dealing with uncertainty. Focus on all those things that are within your control and avoid dwelling on things that are out of your control.

Accept uncertainty and learn to be comfortable if you are dealing with uncertainty. How do you do that? What would be the worst thing that could happen? Sometimes the worst may not be as bad as you may think. Consider uncertainty as an opportunity to grow and learn something new. Whenever a situation is uncertain, treat it as an occasion to learn and be intrigued.

Another way to look at uncertainty is that it is in the future since the event has not happened yet. Worrying about the future does not make sense when it is not here yet. We must accept the past since we cannot change it. We only have this moment to make conscious choices. How would you feel if you could be present now and control what you can to make the best, authentic decision? What actions could you create and follow through? Keep in mind that you can always revise things as you see fit.

No one knows with certainty what the future will bring. Think about your authentic decisions and their consequences. Reflect on past successes whenever moments of uncertainty come your way. You probably had to overcome some of these stressful events in the past. What introspection helped you or made it successful for you? Remember to be in the moment when the time comes.

## *Inflexibility*

In life unpredictability is the norm, so it is in our best interest to be adaptable in the face of change. Inflexible people want things to go as planned, follow a routine, or have some setup. They get upset when things do not follow the path they expected. They feel ill-prepared to deal with unexpected challenges. They find switching from one task to another hard. They must build themselves up for any task they have to do, which is why that predictability is important to them.

This causes stress because things rarely go how we want them to. For example, you might have a perfect day planned and find out your child is sick. Now those plans are ruined because you must take the child to the doctor or spend time caring for your sick child.

If you're facing the unexpected, can you modify your expectations as you go? What do we need to do to overcome inflexibility? You need to realize that the discomfort you feel when plans change goes away once you are engaged with what's happening in the moment. Remind yourself of this and that you will adapt. Think with agility and flexibility by looking at multiple variables and ways of dealing with the unexpected. Life is constantly changing, and accepting that opens us to change and looking for better opportunities.

I used to tell my children that every day is an adventure, a journey to be enjoyed, not a destination. In my practice, staff used to interrupt to ask me if they could add a patient for an urgent matter when we were fully booked. As my clinic got busier, I decided to have a few patient slots for urgent cases. We would use those slots as time to catch up if we did not need them for emergencies. My staff liked the fact that they could handle calls without interrupting the clinical staff, and we had more grateful patients. The patients appreciated that we were accommodating and could make appointments on the same day for urgent needs.

## *Perfectionism*

Perfectionism is not about those who strive for excellence in a healthy way. Some people take genuine pleasure in trying to meet high standards. For example, if you are a high performer, you have high expectations for yourself that you reach to the best of your abilities. Being a high achiever is a good thing.

On the other hand, perfectionism that comes from self-doubt and fears of rejection and disapproval is not healthy. Stress and anxiety can build up when you do not meet high standards or fear that you won't.

There are several kinds of unhealthy perfectionism. Self-oriented perfectionism puts irrational importance on perfection and unrealistic expectations of oneself. Socially prescribed perfectionism leads people to believe they must be perfect to receive approval from others. Lastly, others-oriented perfectionism happens when individuals impose unrealistic standards on people around them and evaluate them critically (Christian 2019).

Perfectionists constantly feel pressure to perform or prove to themselves or others what they can do. It may feel like you have a constant burden on your shoulders. Self-compassion can help you move beyond your mistakes and see challenges as valuable opportunities for growth.

## *Pessimism*

Pessimism is always having a negative outlook on things and expecting the worst to happen to an unrealistic or exaggerated degree. With that mindset, it is hard to see solutions, enact change, or show tenacity in the face of challenges. Pessimism is defeatist, and it saps your energy. Pessimism has been linked to anxiety, depression, sleep disorders, and cardiovascular diseases. It is a dangerous internal stressor.

How do you deal with pessimism? Accept the fact that you cannot change the past, and you cannot control the future since it has not arrived yet. You can do something now. Be fully present to assess your situation and make things happen now. Start with small steps toward what you want. Look at the facts only. Do you have any illogical or irrational thoughts? Pause to develop a better response and not just react.

**CHAPTER 9**

# Skills to Continually Grow Your Authentic Self

*I have not failed. I've just found 10,000 ways that won't work.*
—Thomas Edison

Self-empowerment will lead to a happy life. There are a few markers of a self-empowered approach: (a) understanding where you are and where you would like to be in terms of your needs and desires, (b) setting goals and understanding how to achieve them, and (c) creating strategies to work toward desired outcomes.

To be the best version of yourself, you will need some skills, like a mastery mindset, setting goals, and building resilience for yourself. You need to exercise your wishes by saying no to distractions along the way. A mastery mindset is a kind of growth mindset to continuously develop into the best person you can be. Achieving goals is important to gain confidence.

HAPPY SUCCESSFUL YOU

*I am building self-care, resilience, and endurance!*

## Mastery Mindset

A mastery mindset helps you learn and grow from your mistakes. Striving for mastery can have setbacks and obstacles, making the journey arduous and frustrating. If you gain new knowledge, it will expand your potential. What does a mastery mindset look like? Keeping at your goal until you can do it to the best of your ability. The goal here is not to get to perfection but to become your best.

A mastery mindset is focused on encouraging, learning, and growing. Mastery takes patience, so be patient with yourself. However small your achievement or learning is, you should stop, recognize, and celebrate it.

You are constantly trying to achieve a mastery mindset, although you may never get there. As you get better and move closer to mastery, you are less concerned with the outcome, focusing instead on the process. As you improve, you feel good about achieving mastery. This mindset can show you how to approach life.

The growth mindset, popularized by Carol Dweck, says that everyone can improve and grow through effort and deliberate practice. This idea is more focused on talent and intelligence, which will grow and improve with continuous practice. These mindsets shape how you think about yourself and your world. Your mindset will allow you to envision what success could look like. How you approach your world is not identical to the next person. Setting a goal does not need to be all or none. It can be a variety of shades of gray and silver. You may not recognize your achievements if you do not set goals. Having goals will allow you to seek confirmation toward the life you want.

## Setting Goals

Setting goals is about deciding what you want by setting your intentions and making choices to move toward those goals. Once you have an intention, you can set goals that allow room for learning. Having an overarching goal or a project you are working toward is important. The goal must be specific, reasonable, achievable, time-oriented, and actionable. You can have lifelong goals or short-term goals and everything in between. All that matters is working toward them consistently. Those goals can be broken down into smaller tasks to make the goals more easily achievable.

Understanding what matters to you and what motivates you will allow you to form goals and achieve fulfilling projects. You will find it easier to work toward and sustain long-term projects. Be clear about what you want and why you want it, and form a goal that aligns with those interests.

People can get distracted or overwhelmed by being too busy, and they forget to live with intentionality. They go on autopilot or try to survive the next day. Nothing about that situation improves your well-being.

Goals should be motivating, meaningful, and well-intended. Writing them down can help clarify and articulate what you want. What outcome are you looking for? How will you know when you achieve it? You cannot achieve success when you do not even recognize it. What do you mean by success? How do you want success to look, feel, hear, taste, and smell?

> **Understanding what matters to you and what motivates you will allow you to form goals and achieve fulfilling projects.**

If you get behind on a lofty goal, you may give up because it feels too challenging or you cannot see the end. You can break the goal into smaller pieces to do daily, weekly, or monthly. On the other hand, if your goals are too easy and not challenging enough, they may not engage you.

Why do our goals fail, or why do we not achieve them? There are four common categories: lack of intention, lack of desire, fear of failure, and fear of success. If your goals do not succeed, you may want to examine them more deeply.

There are multiple types and ways of goal setting. I present my goals with 1, 2, and 3, three different goals in a similar arena: (1) is the ideal goal you want to achieve, (2) is an alternate or more accessible goal, and

(3) is what you could learn through the experience to make things easier the second time around. The idea here is similar to the mastery mindset that you cannot fail if you learn something.

An example is looking for a new job that is a better fit than your current job: (1) is to attain a great job with good pay, (2) is a job with the potential to grow into that ideal job, and (3) is that the process of applying and interviewing taught you more about what you want and how to get it. You may feel that you have not learned anything. However, thinking more deeply can help you do better next time. You are much better off having the experience than someone who has not gone through the process.

## Resilience

Resilience is the ability to withstand and recover quickly from adversity. It is the psychological strength you need to overcome challenges. Resilient people are better at rebuilding and carrying on with their lives after difficult times. The more resilient you are, the better you can deal with and overcome stress and burnout. It can even prevent stress and burnout from happening in the first place. You can learn resilience. Many of the skills in this chapter will add to your resilience.

Change is a part of life, and we can control how we respond to it. Being self-aware and adopting the mastery mindset are the first steps toward building resilience. When you fail, you need to learn from your mistakes and failures. Look at failure as an opportunity for growth. You will need passion and perseverance to have a positive outlook and choose your responses proactively to avoid making the same mistakes. Embrace challenges to keep improving.

Building resilience takes small, gradual behavior changes. Avoiding difficult people and situations is not effective. Instead seek situations that are joyful, meaningful, and engaging. For example, avoiding stressful or difficult work will not make you more resilient; taking up challenging, meaningful, and engaging work will allow you to build resilience. Remember that failure is an opportunity to grow and plan to respond differently next time.

Rely on your support system, like family, friends, and colleagues. Know that you are not alone and find some like-minded people. Helping others can be empowering as well.

**Learn to Say No**
When you overcommit, you can get overwhelmed. Sometimes people take on too much in their personal and professional lives, increasing their risk of stress. Taking on just enough is an act of self-care that is also good for your sustained productivity. This means you have to say no at times. Some people grow up being taught that it is rude to say no, but sometimes you

have to say no to protect yourself. You must be honest about your limits and learn to say no.

There are a few ways to say no. The common way is to refuse outright to do something. A good way to do this is to point to a prior commitment. For instance, if your boss asks you to stay late on Friday. You can tell them you have a family commitment that you cannot miss. Instead of just saying no, you can also make a counteroffer, such as staying late on Monday. If your boss wants you to come in on the weekend, you could tell them you cannot, but you can stay an extra hour the following week to help. You can also offer to do a part of what is asked, such as doing the requested work but from home instead of the office. These show your enthusiasm for work while communicating your needs (Zahariades 2017).

Lastly, we have a categorical no. Categorical no is about saying no to some category of tasks or activities. The most helpful way to think about them is to think of them as rules you make for yourself. It is things like not going to bars on weeknights or not answering work emails on weekends. It is a rule you have for yourself that everybody else must respect. If someone invited you for drinks on a Wednesday, you would tell them you do not go out on weeknights.

Remember that saying no to something is saying yes to other things in life. You recognize your precious resources, time, and energy for your well-being. First, thank the person for asking. Communicate your intentions, while being assertive and respectful. It is also good to think about things before answering, if necessary. Ask yourself whether you have the time and energy. Do I have time to rest and recharge? Will this opportunity add value to my life? Understanding yourself, your mental well-being, and mental clarity are vital.

## Deal with Stress

My favorite strategy for dealing with stress is the four *A*s: acknowledge, ask, act, and advance. This strategy works well for acute stress that comes on suddenly or episodic stress that occurs occasionally or irregularly. If you have chronic stress, these strategies are less effective, as chronic stress can change with time.

*Acknowledge* you are experiencing acute or episodic stress. Do not ignore it, and do not keep pushing yourself. When you ignore a problem, you allow it to fester. Problems do not go away because you pretend they do not exist. Acknowledging an episode of stress is like locking onto a target. You cannot take the next critical steps without it.

*Ask* specific questions about the stress you are experiencing. Is this important to you to fix it? If it is a small thing, let it go. What are your options? What is the issue or the specific problem? Be as specific as possible as to the cause of the stress.

*Act* to address it. Create solutions based on what you want. What outcome are you looking for? Think of all potential solutions and select the best one for you. When creating solutions, ask yourself: What responsibility, if any, should you take? What opportunities are there? What connection or relationship could you make? Seek expert help or any other help you need. Know your options, investigate, and take the best action.

*Advance* and move on. If you need time to refine your solution, take it. Build on your previous progress. Periodically revisit solutions to refine them.

For example, I had difficulty picking up my child after my afternoon clinic. I ran about fifteen minutes late, and my child was the last to get picked up. I thought about different solutions, such as eliminating the last patient slot so I could finish early. However, as a junior woman faculty, I did not want to be seen as slacking off. The best solution was to start my clinic earlier to finish fifteen minutes early, but I needed help. I asked the front desk manager for permission to start early to ensure someone could check in patients. I asked my technician if they could be available to start early. My technician and I worked more effectively and efficiently on those days in unspoken teamwork as we completed our patient work. When I could leave the clinic earlier, I was able to be on time for pickup.

## Optimism

Optimism is hopefulness and confidence about an endeavor's future or success (Seligman 2006). Optimistic people perform better in the workplace in challenging situations and report better physical health. Optimists think of adverse situations as temporary, find external forces to blame, and believe that failure in one area does not affect their other abilities.

Let us discuss a few strategies for growing optimism. First, separate facts from judgment, emotion, and interpretation. If you are having any negative thoughts, try writing them down. Ask yourself if there is any validity in what you wrote down. Are there any extreme words like *never*, *always*, or *worst*? They give a clue that the statement may not be sound.

Smiling is a powerful way to build optimism. When you smile first, you likely find people smile back at you (Riggio 2012). By greeting people first, you give the other person an opportunity to greet you. It is up to that person to choose to greet you or not. Each time you smile, you affect your brain which releases feel-good neurotransmitters like dopamine, endorphins, and serotonin, which also help relax your body (Riggio 2012). Surround yourself with more optimists who make the best of every situation.

Next, try visualizations. Instead of noticing problems, visualize opportunities as you say to yourself, "Anything is possible." Allow your visualizations to surprise you. Optimists tend to visualize positive situations around them that can put them in a more positive mood. Getting in the habit of imagining nice, good things happening to you can give you an optimistic outlook. You can also imagine your best possible self. An optimistic attitude can make you a healthier, happier, and more well-rounded person who gets sick less often (Glass 2017).

> **When you learn new things or develop new skills, you are more likely to be more optimistic about life.**

Create a positive mantra. Think of three positive words to inspire you to be more hopeful. Saying those words to yourself will help. Just try it. I used to say, "Be open, curious, and hopeful." Other options could be optimistic, generous, and cheerful. Come up with your own and write them down.

Focus on your successes and learn new things. When you learn new things or develop new skills, you are more likely to be more optimistic about life. Optimism brings new perspectives and shapes your perception of the world.

# Part IV

# The Ultimate Human Goal

Authentic Happiness theory synthesizes all three of traditional theories of happiness (Seligman 2003). They are (1) hedonism, in which a happy life maximizes feelings of pleasure and minimizes pain; (2) Desire theory, which holds that happiness is a matter of getting what you want, sometimes called the "good life"; and (3) Objective List theory, which believes that happiness consists of a life that achieves certain "truly valuable" things in the world, also called a "meaningful life" (Nussbaum 1992). Although the first two are subjective, the third item can be more objective as well.

Most people know what happiness is and yet comparatively few people experience it daily. Why is happiness so elusive? Some people believe that it is out of their control. Some people think that happiness will come when they achieve something, such as getting a new job, new relationship, or good fortune or luck, which can sound too challenging to obtain.

What if happiness was within reach for everyone? You will get various answers when you ask people what happiness means to them. Happiness has different definitions for different people. The most frequent words associated with happiness are love, family, joy, health, well-being, and satisfaction (Hugo 2023). Although we all instinctively know when we are happy, explaining it to someone else is difficult.

As you can see here, defining happiness can get rather complicated. The key to happiness is how you define it for yourself. In this section we'll explore what happiness means to each individual and how to make it a reality in your life.

# CHAPTER 10

# Understanding Happiness

*Happiness is the experience of joy, contentment, or positive well-being, combined with a sense that one's life is good, meaningful, and worthwhile.*

—Sonja Lyubomirsky

There are many ways to view happiness, but the most important thing is to have a clear sense of what happiness means to you, so that you can pursue what makes you happy. Let's explore a few ideas about what happiness means to help you as you refine your own understanding of happiness. What brings happiness to one individual may not necessarily apply to another. Furthermore, happiness is not a constant state but a dynamic and evolving experience influenced by many factors.

HAPPY SUCCESSFUL YOU

*What is happiness if it is not this?*

## Happiness According to Aristotle

The Greek philosopher Aristotle founded the concept that everything, including people, has an essence. He said that essence was created before existence and that people are born with the essence or, in this case, predetermined purpose. The essence described in philosophy is the collection of properties or attributes that make an entity or substance what it fundamentally is, which it has by necessity, and without which it loses its identity (Cartwright 1968). According to essentialism, daily decisions contribute to your ultimate purpose. If you agree with this philosophy, then your purpose or the meaning of life is already created for you.

In contrast to existentialism, where existence precedes essence, essentialism is the opposite. Essentialism believes that essence was created before existence. Since existentialism is based on the concept that there is no essence for humankind, it allows you to create your own meaning and purpose. This concept empowers individuals to find their own essence. For some, it can lead to despair as there is no one you can rely on, which has been a longtime criticism of existentialism.

Aristotle began his inquiry by asking himself, what is a good life? For him, the good life is a life that is good for a human being and fulfills the most profound human function. People are to pursue *eudaimonia*, defined as well-being or thriving, basically "happiness." There are two ways of viewing what is good in life: things that are good for something else and those that are good for their own sake. Money is an example of something that is good for something else. We want money because it pays for rent, health, food, and entertainment. Most of the things we want or do are for something else. However, this happiness, or *eudaimonia*, is our human purpose and is pursued for its own sake. Happiness is the only thing we want that is not for something else (Moore 2019). In other words, you want happiness for its own sake, not because it would get you anything else.

What does Aristotle mean by happiness? As translated in English, *eudaimonia* is not a hedonistic state, like a mental state of joy or pleasure. It requires virtues. Although Aristotelian happy life may include moments of happiness and contentment as conventionally understood, it also involves the exercise of mental faculties unique to the human mind, such as self-transcendence. Self-transcendence means looking beyond oneself and adopting a more extensive view that includes concern for others. Aristotelian happiness is a way of living and thriving, and happiness is the end of human endeavor.

Aristotle's most influential work was a moral treatise on Nicomachean Ethics. He discusses the doctrine of the mean, sometimes known as the golden mean, which states that every virtue in excellence is the mean or the middle of the two extremes. In addition, every virtue is about being rational and dispositional in a continuum of two extremes (Aristotle 2011). The critical point in understanding Aristotle is that he is not necessarily prescribing how to be virtuous but describing when we are being virtuous. Rational activities are not only intellectual, like philosophy. They also include all things that rely on human intellect and rationality (things unique to the human brain), like courage, temperance, charity, magnificence, magnanimity, patience, truthfulness, wittiness, friendliness, ambition, and justice.

For example, in the virtue of courage, we face two extremes: having too much courage, almost recklessness, and not enough courage, meaning a person who cannot act. You need some courage, which is the goal, but your choice of how much you will need will differ in different situations. There are no right or wrong answers. Therefore, moral virtue is formed through action and habituation; good action requires prudence.

What does it mean to achieve excellence in those areas? Excellence is achieving an appropriate competency related to one's life or goals. It is a process and involves balance. For instance, you cannot be smothering or distant if you want to be a great friend. You need to find a middle ground, being sensitive to the other person's needs and your own. There is no correct answer. You must know what is appropriate for each situation; that point of excellence is usually between two extremes. This approach requires you to assess your circumstances. What is your goal, and what is your best response?

> **Happiness is a creative process because you make choices to find ways to flourish in any given situation.**

What are the most critical insights from all of this? Happiness is the continuous attempt to fulfill human nature, spirit, potential, and goals. This tells us that happiness is made up of choices that include many acts and pursuits, and it is the most meaningful way you can live as it aligns with the human spirit. Happiness is a creative process because you make choices to find ways to flourish in any given situation.

If you live pursuing *eudaimonia*, the other attributes we associate with happiness come naturally, like joy, pleasure, and contentment. Many people make the mistake of trying to feel joy and pleasure without living well, which makes all those positive feelings unsustainable because you have yet to create the conditions that sustain them.

At the heart of Aristotle's philosophy is a message of self-empowerment: planning, making choices, and working towards goals that improve your life. "Happiness depends upon ourselves," Aristotle said. It is not a gift other people or things can give us. The ultimate happiness is created from within, and we are responsible for protecting it. What makes you happy is individual and will be different for each person.

## Other Happiness Ideas

Where does happiness come from? Many others have explored this idea since Aristotle's time. For instance, genes and the environment significantly impact happiness. Genes determine a person's eye color, height, academic achievement, success, behavior, personality, health, and happiness. Inherited DNA differences are why we are the way we are. Identical twin studies show that happiness is also inheritable; about 50 percent is from your genetic makeup (Plomin 2019).

Both genes and environmental influences affect each other as they are interdependent. Epigenetics studies show how your environment and behaviors cause DNA to turn genes on and off for expression. Genes and the environment constantly influence each other. For instance, when pregnant mothers experience famine, chemical changes affect their baby's growth factor, meaning their babies are born smaller than usual (Gibney 2021).

Another example of epigenetics is if you are predisposed to love reading, you will fill your environment with reading material, meaning your children grow up in an environment filled with books. Those children will have a higher chance of reading for fun because they inherited that propensity from their parents and their environment is filled with books. Therefore, separating the influences of genetics and the environment is quite difficult.

According to Lyubomirsky, half of our happiness (50 percent) comes from our genetic makeup; our race, ethnicity, and built-in preferences affect behavior, personality, and other traits. Another 40 percent of happiness comes from belief systems, attitudes, interpretations, and mindsets people can choose and explore. Therefore, she emphasizes that this 40 percent is under your control. Only 10 percent comes from your circumstances, such as socioeconomic status (Lyubomirsky 2008).

Psychology suggests that happiness and meaning are the essential elements of well-being. However, pursuing happiness and meaning do not always correlate with each other (Baumeister 2013).

In the next chapter, you will learn that the best science shows happiness is far more in our control than we might think, despite our circumstances. Furthermore, we will explore happiness not as a state of being but as a way of living.

Performing activities that feel natural, enjoyable, and driven by your values brings you more happiness than striving to meet other people's expectations. Choosing activities that are meaningful to you rather than trying to feel good is the key. In addition, adding variety to your routines keeps your brain alive to more possibilities.

**CHAPTER 11**

# Living a Happy Life

*To be oneself, simply oneself, is so amazing and utterly unique an experience that it's hard to convince oneself so singular a thing happens to everybody.*
—Simone de Beauvoir

What would a happy look like for you? Happiness is not a destination but a journey. There is no perfect journey that fits everyone. Each person will view their journey through their own lens, so the meaning may differ, even when two people are experiencing the same situation. This chapter has two parts: first, you'll think through how the dimensions of yourself relate to your happiness; second, we'll explore some habits to increase happiness in your life.

HAPPY SUCCESSFUL YOU

*I am jumping for joy!*

## Dimensions of You

Some dimensions of yourself affect your happiness more than others. I will highlight a few research-based areas. For example, when you are distracted and not engaged, consider why. The reason is generally based on physical, mental, emotional, and social areas.

### *Physical*

Being physically healthy is not just about being free from illness. It also includes having the energy to live a happier life. The tips below will help you stay healthy.

A well-balanced, healthy diet is essential to health and energy. Eating nourishing food to sustain your health will look different for each of us. I am not advocating any particular diet. Figure out what will work best for you and have some fun by mixing it up.

Are you getting adequate sleep? If not, what would it mean for you to prioritize sleep? Most adults need at least six to eight hours of sleep each night. Some may not need as much, but the quality of sleep is important too. What is preventing you from getting the rest you need? Catch up on your sleep now if you cannot get enough sleep every night.

Regular exercise will help your health. According to the US Department of Health and Human Services, adults need 150 minutes of moderate-intensity aerobics or 75 minutes of vigorous activities per week (Laskowski 2021).

## *Mental*

Create something meaningful to you each day. Do you have a unique talent to share, or do you want to practice things you feel passionate about? Simple things like cooking or sharing a healthy meal allow you to do something you enjoy daily. Your effort for things that matter most to you will help bring out the best in you.

Try to declutter your brain once in a while, like spring cleaning. Focus on what you want to see, taste, hear, smell, touch, and do. Focus on what matters to you, and do not worry about things that have not happened yet. Life is unfolding now, so stay in the present moment. Reflect on your work if it brings meaning to you. For example, I have patients who were so happy after refractive surgery, like LASIK, because they can see well without glasses. Just reflecting on those patients is hugely meaningful to me.

## *Emotional*

Create at least one happy moment every day. Your happiest moments likely include laughter, so find reasons to laugh. Choose to watch a funny movie or a comedy show, share a joke, or don't take yourself too seriously. Remember that emotional states are dynamic not constant states. Be flexible and enjoy what you can.

## Social

According to Waldinger and Schultz (2023), relationships contribute to a happier, healthier life. If you enjoy doing activities with others, find someone to join you in what you enjoy. Whether your network consists of family, friends, or coworkers, people are crucial for promoting happiness, reducing stress, and sharing resources when life gets challenging. Building a social circle involves participating in social events, having dinners together, watching movies, visiting museums, or walking together. There are many options.

## Happier Habits

Happiness is a way of life, and habits can add to a happier life. This section focuses on habits you can incorporate into your life to engender happiness. There are many effective methods, such as reflecting on what made you happy before, expressing gratitude, and performing kind acts.

> **Happiness is a way of life, and habits can add to a happier life.**

### Revisiting What Made You Happy Before

Remember the things that used to make you happy. Try going back to the things you used to enjoy that filled your life with fun and happiness. For me, it is playing piano. Although I do not play as well as I used to, I still enjoy it.

Things that make you happy are not distractions. You may not feel up to them. You may even think there is no pleasure to be derived from them. Try again to see if there are any positive feelings left. Remember the things that used to fill your time that you used to look forward to. It does not matter if you have not done them in years or how much you doubt; it may bring you joy. You may be surprised by what emotions show up.

If you used to enjoy watching golf on weekends, start doing that again and see for yourself. If you enjoyed getting lunch with your friend at a nearby coffee shop, how about reviving that tradition? If you used to enjoy reading fiction, stop by the local bookshop and pick up some titles. If playing video games is what you enjoyed, pick up the video game again. If you used to love talking to your child after work, start again. If there are things that used to make you happy, find them and be available for them again.

### *Gratitude*

Practicing gratitude makes you happier by helping you notice the positives in your life. This makes you feel good, improves your mood, and positively affects your health. Here are some tips for practicing gratitude.

Keep a gratitude journal, listing two or three things you are grateful for daily. It does not matter how small or big each item is. Sometimes you may need to look around to find things you take for granted and express gratitude. Journaling helps bring consistency. Do not wait for opportunities to be grateful, seek them out (Emmons 2003).

For instance, you may be grateful that you have a heated home, that the coffee place close to your workplace always has your favorite bagels, and that you have a dog that is always glad to see you. You may be grateful that it rained or did not rain today. You can also be grateful that things did not go as badly as they could have. Whatever you can think of that makes you thankful, jot it down. For the journaling habit to last, make it quite simple. Set a reminder if you want to make it a part of your routine.

Do something that expresses gratitude for something someone has done that you appreciate. It may be recent or in the past. You can write them an email, a letter, or a card to thank them. You can call to thank them and to catch up. If the people you are grateful to are public figures, you can thank them on social media or tell a friend you are thankful for what they have done. If someone is quite remarkable to you, you can visit them and thank them in person, especially when they do something significant. You can do this regularly.

Like a vision board discussed in Chapter 4, you can make a gratitude board that you fill with photos and things for which you are grateful. Make a mental note to express your gratitude whenever you visit the board. Display it somewhere you can easily view it. Continue adding to it as you find more things for which you are grateful.

Expressing your gratitude verbally is straightforward. For instance, you can say, "I am thankful for the trees and the sunny weather." However, you can express your gratitude mentally as well. If you see photos that put a smile on your face or think of someone you love or listen to music that helps you relax, you are showing mental gratitude. There are many more ways to express gratitude. Find yours.

## *Kind Acts*

Doing kind acts for someone makes them happier and, more importantly, makes you happier. Doing kind acts releases hormones that make you feel good. It will boost your serotonin, the neurotransmitter responsible for feelings of satisfaction and well-being. Like exercising, altruism also releases endorphins,

> **Doing kind acts for someone makes them happier and, more importantly, makes you happier.**

making you feel good.

In addition, kindness releases the hormone oxytocin, which causes the release of nitric oxide, dilating the blood vessels, and reducing blood pressure. As mentioned earlier in this book, kindness also helps build relationships with others and decreases stress.

Giving a sincere compliment and saying it with a smile is an easy way to brighten someone's day, including yours.

## *Savoring Experience*

Savoring is all about enjoying an experience to the fullest. It includes stepping out of an experience, reviewing it, and appreciating it while it is happening. It is about heightening your experience of an event, like savoring good food.

Getting into the habit of savoring experiences as they happen increases your overall happiness (Jose 2012). The experience can be anything you find favorable. Savoring a positive experience will deepen your positive emotions. You can savor something by sharing it with people who would also love it, showing emotion, being grateful, and paying attention to how it interacts with your senses. Use all five senses—sight, hearing, smell, taste, and touch—whenever possible.

For instance, if you watch a funny video, you can savor it by sharing it, laughing, being happy you discovered it, and paying attention to all the positive things you feel as you enjoy it. Doing so will deepen the experience, creating a longer-lasting effect, and making you happier overall. Get in the habit of savoring at least one thing every day.

For example, many of my patients get very excited after cataract surgery because their vision improves. The world becomes brighter and clearer for them. When they return in six months or a year, they frequently forget about some of the comments they made before or immediately after the surgery. Savoring that experience by sharing their comments has added to the happiness of the patients, family, and our staff.

## CONCLUSION

*You are the master of your destiny . . .*
*You can make your life what you want it to be.*
— Napoleon Hill

Conscious living is living with intention and choosing to invest and develop to your full potential. Become self-aware and figure out who you are, including what values and principles are essential for you to create meaning. Conscious living is an important part of your reinventing yourself.

Authentic living is a part of conscious living. It is being the best version of yourself, making commitments, and making meaningful connections through kindness, compassion, empathy, and forgiveness. Authenticity considers community, society, and global views because we do not exist alone. Every step of the way, you make the choices you desire.

Creating meaning is a unique quality of being human. We need both happiness and meaning in our lives. Although being happy and having a meaningful life are both critical, there are differences between being happy and having a meaningful life. You can experience happiness without necessarily having a strong sense of meaning in life and vice versa, but happiness and meaningfulness can overlap and influence each other.

Happiness focuses on the present moment and individual well-being, whereas meaningfulness extends beyond immediate experience, encompassing a broader perspective on life. It integrates past, present, and future. Thinking about the future and past is associated with high meaning but low happiness. Happiness is linked to being a taker more than a giver, whereas meaning is associated with being a giver (Baumeister 2013).

Happiness satisfies your needs, gets what you want, and makes you feel good. In this view of happiness, you only consider yourself and no one else. In contrast, meaning is related to uniquely human activities such as developing a personal identity, expressing the self, and consciously integrating the feeling that what you do matters.

How much happiness and meaning we experience depends on us. You make choices for yourself. We all need a balance between happiness and meaning; we need both things to have a fulfilling life.

This book started by looking at alternate views to help you think differently and to create options and opportunities. Remembering your purpose and inventing your meaning at work creates opportunities.

CONCLUSION

Overcoming internal stressors keeps them from limiting you.

You can empower yourself to create your meaning. By forging your purpose, values, and alignment, you can give yourself success. Succeeding in life is about who you are and what you expect to get from life. How would it change your life if you became the person you desired to be? That means you get to know yourself and do not need to follow in anyone else's footsteps.

> **By forging your purpose, values, and alignment, you can give yourself success.**

We are entering the Great Disengagement, an era of fatigue brought about by new coronavirus variants and confusion about people's expectations. It's like quiet quitting, but this is not only in the workplace but everywhere. This disengagement is common at colleges and universities, affecting many young people and their learning communities.

I see this as an opportunity. What outcomes and solutions could you develop to rebuild, recharge, and renormalize your life? Could you come back stronger than you used to be? What is it that we want as a community and a society? Could we do this better in the new normal? What would that look like or feel like once we get there?

We began with philosophical ideas to inspire, grow, and expand our thoughts and viewpoints. I selected concepts that are relevant today. Achieving success and happiness is possible when you love what you are doing and pursue your authentic, best self.

> **Never give up on the steadfast love of learning. There is always more to learn.**

Remember where you started. Where are you now?

- What was your experience in this book?
- What advice would you give yourself?
- What have you learned that you want to remember?
- What is becoming clearer for you?
- What useful insights do you want to see grow after reading this book?

We are all learning. Never give up on the steadfast love of learning. There is always more to learn.

# CALL TO ACTION

### Please Post a Review

If you like what you read in *Happy Successful You: Unleashing a Life of Intentional Choices, Purpose, and Meaning,* please post a review at your favorite online retailer. This will help to reach more people with this message. Thank you!

For more information, please visit my website: ChristineELeeMD.com/books/

# ACKNOWLEDGMENTS

Writing and publishing a book takes tremendous support, as in any worthwhile endeavor. I gratefully acknowledge all my clients and patients for opening up to me, believing in me, sharing their stories freely, showing vulnerability, and inspiring me.

I want to thank my colleagues and my personal and professional friends for their encouraging words and for supporting me as a person and professional throughout my career.

To my stellar peer reviewers, Brian Brooks Combs, Leslie Matsukawa, and Janis Bell Lim, thank you for taking the time to read this manuscript and providing your honest and valuable feedback. You helped shape this book into what it is today.

To Christine Kloser, Carrie Jareed, and the rest of the editorial and production team at Capucia Publishing for their dedication and professionalism.

I want to acknowledge and thank my mom for her inspiration, for fostering my desire to be the best version of myself, and for the dedicated love I feel whenever I speak to her. I also want to acknowledge my siblings, Cathy, Alex, and Athena, for their support and love.

To my loving family, especially my three amazing adult children, Ted, Matthew, and Michelle, for your brilliant minds, creative spirit, and amazing energy.

To my dearest husband, Michael, for being the enduring source of light, tirelessly encouraging me, being the greatest cheerleader, and standing next to me through all the ups and downs of life. Thank you so much for loving me.

# REFERENCES

Abramson, Ashley. 2022. "Burnout and Stress Are Everywhere." *American Psychological Association* 53 (1): 72.

Achor, Shawn, Andrew Reece, Gabriella Kellerman, and Alexi Robichaux. 2018. "9 Out of 10 People Are Willing to Earn Less Money to Do More-Meaningful Work." *Harvard Business Review*. 06 November. hbr.org/2018/11/9-out-of-10-people-are-willing-to-earn-less-money-to-do-more-meaningful-work

Aristotle. 2011. *Aristotle's Nicomachean Ethics*. Translated by Robert Bartlett and Susan Collins. Chicago: The University of Chicago Press.

Bailey, Catherine, and Adrian Madden. 2016. "What Makes Work Meaningful—Or Meaningless?" *MIT Sloan Management Review*. 01 June. sloanreview.mit.edu/article/what-makes-work-meaningful-or-meaningless

Bakewell, Sarah. 2016. *At the Existentialist Café: Freedom, Being, and Apricot Cocktails*. New York: Other Press.

Bamford, Rebecca. 2019. "The Relevance of Existentialism." *The Philosophers' Magazine* 84: 77–81.

Baumeister, Roy, Kathleen Vohs, Jennifer Aaker, and Emily Garbinsky. 2013. "Some Key Differences Between a Happy Life and a Meaningful Life." *The Journal of Positive Psychology* 8 (6): 505–516.

Beauvoir, Simone de. 1992. *The Prime of Life: The Autobiography of Simone de Beauvoir, 1929-1944*. Cleveland, OH: World Publishing Company.

Bravata, Dena, Divya Madhusudhan, Michael Boroff, and Kevin Cokley. 2020. "Commentary: Prevalence, Predictors, and Treatment of Imposter Syndrome: A Systematic Review." *Journal of Mental Health & Clinical Psychology.* 24 August. www.mentalhealthjournal.org/articles/commentary-prevalence-predictors-and-treatment-of-imposter-syndrome-a-systematic-review.html

Buckingham, Marcus. 2007. *Go Put Your Strengths to Work: 6 Powerful Steps to Achieve Outstanding Performance.* New York: Free Press, Division of Simon & Schuster, Inc.

Cairns, Rebecca. 2021. "5 Ways to Recover from Burnout at Work." *Insider.* 19 November. www.insider.com/guides/health/mental-health/burnout

Camus, Albert. 1955. *The Myth of Sisyphus*, 2018 translation edition. New York: Vintage International, Random House.

Cartwright, Richard. 1968. "Some Remarks on Essentialism." *The Journal of Philosophy* 65 (20): 615–626.

Christian, Lyn. 2019. "Overcoming: Don't Let Perfect Be the Enemy of Good." *SoulSalt.* 29 October. soulsalt.com/overcoming-perfectionism

Doyle, Alison. 2022. "What Is the Average Number of Work Hours Per Week?" *The Balance.* 07 September. www.thebalancemoney.com/what-is-the-average-hours-per-week-worked-in-the-us-2060631

Duignan, Brian. 2019. "Eudaimonia | Greek Philosophy" *Encyclopedia Britannica.* www.britannica.com/topic/eudaimonia

Dunn, Elizabeth. 2014. *Happy Money: The Science of Happier Spending.* New York: Simon & Schuster.

# REFERENCES

Elflein, John. 2019. "Percentage of US Employees Who Stated the Stress from their Job Caused Them to Regularly Engage in Unhealthy Behaviors from 2015 to 2017, by Industry." *Statista*. 14 January. www.statista.com/statistics/807091/work-stress-causing-unhealthy-behaviors-us-by-industry

Ellerbeck, Stefan. 2023. "The Great Resignation Continues. Why Are US Workers Continuing to Quit their Jobs?" *World Economic Forum*. 25 January. www.weforum.org/agenda/2023/01/us-workers-jobs-quit

Emmons, Robert, and Michael McCullough. 2003. "Counting Blessings vs. Burdens: An Experimental Investigation of Gratitude and Subjective Well-Being in Daily Life." *Journal of Personality and Social Psychology* 84 (2): 377–389.

Eurich, Tasha. 2017. *Insight: Why We're Not as Self-Aware as We Think, and How Seeing Ourselves Clearly Helps Us Succeed at Work and in Life*. New York: Random House.

Eurich, Tasha. 2018. "What Self-Awareness Really Is (and How to Cultivate It)." *Harvard Business Review*. 04 January. hbr.org/2018/01/what-self-awareness-really-is-and-how-to-cultivate-it

Finkelstein, Bianca. 2021. "3 Ways to Let Passion Ignite your Career." *Fast Company*. 01 June. www.fastcompany.com/90641368/3-ways-to-let-passion-ignite-your-career-without-burning-it-down

Gibney, E.R., and C.M. Nolan. 2010. "Epigenetics and Gene Expression." *Heredity* 105: 4–13. 12 May. www.nature.com/articles/hdy201054#citeas

Glass, Jeremy. 2017. "Having an Optimistic Outlook Can Benefit Your Life—Here's How." *Mashable*. 04 August. mashable.com/ad/article/optimistic-outlook-can-benefit-life

Gotter, Ana. 2017. "Racing Thoughts: Tips for Coping." *Healthline.* 19 June. www.healthline.com/health/racing-thoughts

Greene, Jessica. 2019. "Work on Your Strengths, Not Your Weaknesses." *Zapier.* 09 May. zapier.com/blog/how-to-find-your-strengths

Habib, Marianne, Mathieu Cassotti, Sylvain Moutier, Olivier Houde, and Olivier Borst. 2015. "Fear and Anger Have Opposite Effects on Risk Seeking in the Gain Frame." *Frontier Psychology.* 10 March. www.frontiersin.org/articles/10.3389/fpsyg.2015.00253/full

Haybron, Dan. 2020. "Happiness." *Stanford Encyclopedia of Philosophy.* 28 May. plato.stanford.edu/entries/happiness

Hill, Napoleon. 2004. *Think and Grow Rich: The Landmark Bestseller Revised and Updated for the 21st Century.* New York: Penguin Group.

Hugo. 2023. "What Does Happiness Mean to You? (1,155 Answers with 11 Examples)." *Tracking Happiness.* 29 January. www.trackinghappiness.com/what-happiness-means-to-you

Iacurci, Greg. 2023. "2022 was the Real Year of the Great Resignation says Economist." *CNBC.* 01 February. www.cnbc.com/2023/02/01/why-2022-was-the-real-year-of-the-great-resignation.html

Jose, Paul, Bee Lim, and Fred Bryant. 2012. "Does Savoring Increase Happiness? A Daily Diary Study." *Journal of Positive Psychology* 7 (3): 176–187.

Kane, Leslie. 2022. "Physician Burnout & Depression Report: Stress, Anxiety, and Anger." www.medscape.com/slideshow/2022-lifestyle-burnout-6014664?icd=login_success_email_match_norm

"Kierkegaard, Søren." *Wikipedia.* en.wikipedia.org/wiki/Søren_Kierkegaard.

# REFERENCES

Landau, Iddo. 2017. *Finding Meaning in an Imperfect World.* New York: Oxford University Press.

Laskowski, Edward. 2021. "How Much Should the Average Adult Exercise Every Day?" *Mayo Clinic.* 16 June. www.mayoclinic.org/healthy-lifestyle/fitness/expert-answers/exercise/faq-20057916

Lyubomirsky, Sonja. 2008. *The How of Happiness: A Scientific Approach to Getting the Life You Want.* New York: Penguin Press.

Lyubomirsky, Sonja. 2005. "Pursuing Happiness: The Architecture of Sustainable Change." *Review of General Psychology* 9 (2): 111–131.

Martela, Frank, and Michael Steger. 2016. "The Three Meanings in Life: Distinguishing Coherence, Purpose, and Significance." *The Journal of Positive Psychology* 11 (5): 531-545.

Maslach, Christina, and M.P. Leiter. 2016. "Burnout" from *Stress: Concepts, Cognition, Emotion, and Behavior.* Cambridge: Academic Press. 351–357. doi.org/10.1016/b978-0-12-800951-2.00044-3

McDonald, William. 2023. "Soren Kierkegaard." *The Internet Encyclopedia of Philosophy. Kierkegaard.* https://iep.utm.edu/kierkega

McQuaid, Michelle. 2014. "Ten Reasons to Focus on Your Strengths." *Psychology Today.* 11 November. www.psychologytoday.com/us/blog/functioning-flourishing/201411/ten-reasons-focus-your-strengths

Mehrabian, Albert. 1972. *Silent Messages.* Belmont, CA: Wadsworth Publishing Company.

Middleton, Kym. 2016. "What is the Sunlight Test." *Ethics Explainer.* 08 September. ethics.org.au/ethics-explainer-the-sunlight-test

Minhaz, Muntasir. 2023. "Money as a Motivator: Can Money Motivate Employees?" *iEduNote.* www.iedunote.com/money-motivator

Moore, Catherine. 2019. "What is Eudaimonia? Aristotle and Eudaimonic Well-Being." *Positive Psychology.* 08 April. positivepsychology.com/eudaimonia

Newport, Cal. 2022. "The Year in Quiet Quitting." *The New Yorker.* 29 December. www.newyorker.com/culture/2022-in-review/the-year-in-quiet-quitting

Nussbaum, Martha. 1992. "Human Functioning and Social Justice: In Defense of Aristotelian Essentialism." *Political Theory* 20: 202–246

Otake, Keiko, Shimai Satoshi, Junko Tanaka-Matumi, Kanako Otsui, Barbara Frederickson. 2006. "Happy People Become Happier through Kindness: A Counting Kindnesses Intervention." *Journal of Happiness Studies* 7 (3): 361–375.

Plomin, Robert. 2019. *Blueprint: How DNA Makes Us Who We Are.* New York: Penguin Books.

Riggio, Ronald. 2012. "There's Magic in Your Smile." *Psychology Today.* 25 June. www.psychologytoday.com/us/blog/cutting-edge-leadership/201206/there-s-magic-in-your-smile

Sartre, Jean-Paul. 1946. *Existentialism Is a Humanism.* New Haven, CT: Yale University Press.

Saymeh, Amal. 2023. "What Is Imposter Syndrome? Learn What It Is and 10 Ways to Cope." *BetterUp.* 22 February. www.betterup.com/blog/what-is-imposter-syndrome-and-how-to-avoid-it

Seligman, Martin, Tracy A. Steen, Nansook Park, and Christopher Peterson. 2005. "Positive Psychology Progress: Empirical Validation of Interventions." *American Psychologist Journal* 60 (5): 410–21.

# REFERENCES

Seligman, Martin. 2006. *Learned Optimism*. New York: Vintage Books.

Seligman, Martin. 2005. *Authentic Happiness*. New York: Free Press.

Segal, Jeanne, Melinda Smith, and Lawrence Robinson. 2023. "Stress Symptoms, Signs, and Causes." www.helpguide.org/articles/stress/stress-symptoms-signs-and-causes.htm

Siegle, Steve. 2020. "The Art of Kindness." *Mayo Clinic Health System*. 29 May. www.mayoclinichealthsystem.org/hometown-health/speaking-of-health/the-art-of-kindness

Star, Katharina. 2019. "Overcoming All-or-Nothing Thinking When You Have Anxiety Issues." *Verywell Mind*. www.verywellmind.com/all-or-nothing-thinking-2584173

Threlkeld, Kristy. 2021. "Employee Burnout Report: COVID-19's Impact and 3 Strategies to Curb It." *Indeed*. 11 March. www.indeed.com/lead/preventing-employee-burnout-report

Tulshyan, Rushika and Jodi-Ann Burey. 2021. "Stop Telling Women They Have Imposter Syndrome." *Harvard Business Review*. 11 February. hbr.org/2021/02/stop-telling-women-they-have-imposter-syndrome

Turner, Ashley. 2019. "The World Health Organization Officially Recognizes Workplace 'Burnout' as an Occupational Phenomenon." *CNBC*. 28 May. www.cnbc.com/2019/05/28/who-recognizes-workplace-burnout-as-an-occupational-phenomenon.html

United States Bureau of Labor and Statistics. 2023. "Average Hours Employed People Spent Working on Days Worked by Day of Week." *American Time Use Survey Summary*. 22 June. www.bls.gov/charts/american-time-use/emp-by-ftpt-job-edu-h.htm

Waldinger, Robert, and Marc Schulz. 2023. *The Good Life: Lessons from the World's Longest Scientific Study of Happiness*. New York: Simon & Schuster.

Wooll, Maggie. 2021. "You Know You Need Human Connection. Here's How to Achieve It." *BetterUp*. 17 November. www.betterup.com/blog/human-connection

Wooll, Maggie, 2022. "Don't Let Limiting Beliefs Hold You Back. Learn to Overcome Yours." *BetterUp*. 19 July. www.betterup.com/blog/what-are-limiting-beliefs

Zahariades, Damon. 2017. *The Art of Saying No*. www.artofproductivity.com

Zak, Heidi. 2020. "Adults Make More Than 35,000 Decisions per Day. Here Are 4 Ways to Prevent Mental Burnout." *Inc.com*. 21 January. www.inc.com/heidi-zak/adults-make-more-than-35000-decisions-per-day-here-are-4-ways-to-prevent-mental-burnout.html

# CONTACT THE AUTHOR

**Address:**
Christine E. Lee, MD, CPE, PCC
Houston, TX

**Website:**
www.christineleemd.com

**Social:**
Linkedin.com/in/christine-lee-md-pcc/
Facebook.com/christine.lee.md
Twitter.com/Leemdwellness

## ABOUT THE AUTHOR

Christine E Lee, MD, CPE, PCC, stands out in health care, where science and compassion intertwine. She is a board-certified, comprehensive ophthalmologist specializing in cataract and refractive surgery. As the CEO of Crossroads Coaching & Consulting, she merges her medical expertise with that of an executive professional coach.

Dr. Lee's academic journey traces back to the University of Michigan honors program, where she majored in Philosophy and Cellular and Molecular Biology. She earned her MD from the University of Michigan Medical School. Her journey continued with an ophthalmology residency at the University of Virginia, solidifying her expertise in the field. She started as a Medical Scientist Training Program MD-PhD candidate during medical school; however, she instead became a Howard Hughes Research Scholar and spent a year at the National Institutes of Health (NIH) researching in the Molecular Immunology Section.

Dr. Lee is a lifelong learner with an impressive roster of certifications, reflecting her commitment to personal and professional growth. The International Coaching Federation bestowed her with the Professional Certified Coach (PCC) designation. She also received the Certified Professional Coach (CPC) credential, the Energy Leadership Index Master Practitioner (ELIMP) title, and the COR.E Leadership Dynamic Specialist (CLDS) distinction from the Institute of Professional Excellence in Coaching. Dr. Lee pursued the Certified Physician Executive (CPE) designation through the American Association of Physician Leadership.

At the core of Dr. Lee's remarkable achievements is a leadership philosophy built on integrity, trust, and respect. With a background in philosophy, she brings a unique strategic perspective, deftly considering multiple viewpoints and fostering collaboration across disciplines. She charts a course toward excellence and happiness for herself and helps others do the same.

Dr. Lee's personal life adds fulfillment and joy to her life. She shares her life's journey with her beloved husband, Michael Y. Lee, MD, forging a partnership that celebrates love and companionship. Together, they raised three incredible children, Ted, Matthew, and Michelle, who have blossomed into successful adults.

Made in the USA
Middletown, DE
22 February 2024